THE HOT BOOK OF
Chillies

Special thanks go to Derryck Strachan (Ashburton Cookery School) and Chilli Pepper Pete (retailer of fine dried chillies and hot spicy pickles), who put up with my questions and visits, as well as Andy Teo whose cooking is always a delight to sample. Most of all I wish to thank my wife, Sonia, and my family – Nick, Jason, Lizzi and Antony – who have tasted and tested countless recipes, and my mother, Edna, without whom there would have been many more mistakes in the text.

THE HOT BOOK OF
Chillies

DAVID FLOYD

Contents

The chilli story

This story starts in the jungles of the Amazon, original home of a plant that produces a naturally powerful alkaloid compound. The plant has been spread so diligently that it can now be found on every continent and, although it was virtually unknown outside South America before 1492, it is now common in many parts of the world. On the Indian subcontinent and in the Far East, its use is viewed as indispensable to daily life. In fact, so well has it been accepted here that many assume it is native to this region.

Initially spread by birds, it is humans who took over as the main carriers, developing and spreading the chilli as they moved around the planet. Those who come into contact with it report uncontrollable physical symptoms including sweating, runny noses and coughing – all of these surprisingly culminating in a general feeling of wellbeing. Its victims soon feel the need to partake of its delights again, but find they need ever-increasing quantities to regain that initial sensation and satisfy their craving.

Right: Red, green, yellow or purple; long or slender, short or round, twisted or smooth; fresh, dried, raw or cooked – the versatility of chilli pods invites experimentation and promises many culinary adventures.

A good all-rounder

Chilli farming and distribution has become big business, making some individuals both influential and rich. In most countries you will find devotees growing chillies for their own consumption. They are available in many forms, including fresh, dried, or powdered, as an oleoresin (see page 27), or in the form of a hot sauce. Some varieties are hot- or cold-smoked before use. Many fanatics carry them around with them so that they can enjoy their pleasures at any meal, wherever they may be. In their purified state chillies were used as an effective weapon in close combat, yet they can also provide relief from pain.

Chillies are simple to grow and available everywhere. And although the fruits are capable of causing the most severe discomfort, they have become one of the world's most popular spices.

Left: Nature's Christmas ornaments – chillies not only taste great, they make very attractive ornamental shrubs.

What is a chilli?

The genus *Capsicum* is said to have evolved in a corner of South America that is bordered by Bolivia, Brazil, Paraguay and Argentina. It is here that the greatest number of wild species grow. The chilli counts among its family members such species as the potato, tobacco and even the deadly nightshade (*Atropa belladonna*). Along with over 3000 others it forms part of the Solanaceae family.

The word 'chilli' is a legacy of South American civilizations who knew the plants and cultivated different varieties. 'Pepper', the confusing alternative, was introduced by Columbus whose voyage took him to South America. So steadfast was he in his belief that he had secured a Spanish trade route to the spices of India that he misnamed the pungent, red chilli pods.

Bell peppers and chillies are related, however, and very similar, except that only the chilli produces the chemical capsaicin which gives it ists pungent taste. So closely related are the two that if you grow chilli and pepper varieties in close proximity they will cross-pollinate. Seeds harvested from peppers that have been crossed will taste hot – in other words the chilli gene will dominate. Plant breeders and seed companies go to great lengths to keep their seed lines pure. Any seeds you procure from a home garden should be viewed with suspicion. You won't know what you get until the plants begin to produce fruit.

Today, chillies and peppers are grown commercially in over 80 countries. The largest harvests come from China, Indonesia, Korea, Mexico, Nigeria and Turkey – a combined harvesting area not far short of 800,000ha (3000 square miles). Though mostly grown in warm climes, even the UK has over 100ha (247 acres) of chillies; France over 1000ha (2471 acres). Production of chillies is booming to satisfy a growing demand.

The chilli is often described as 'addictive', but not in a negative sense like tobacco, for instance, since no deep craving develops and there is no chemical dependency. It is true, however, that the warming, burning sensation we get from chillies stimulates the release of endorphins – natural painkillers that also create a feeling of wellbeing. It is therefore quite possible that the enjoyment of chillies is linked to a subconscious desire for this pleasant state of wellbeing. Sadly, over time, the tolerance to capsaicin increases and we need more or hotter chillies to produce the same sensation.

Escape from the jungle

Little is known about chillies before 1492, when Columbus brought the first specimens back to Europe. In her book *Peppers, the Domesticated Capsicums*, Jean Andrews speculates on, and maps out, the probable origin of the species to an area of central Bolivia. It is safe to surmise that the plants originated in the jungles of South America, and that the fruits with their fiery taste are an adaptation designed to ward off the attentions of hungry mammals. Birds cannot taste spicy flavours and would not have been affected. For them, the wild chillies were a good source of food and thus they spread the seeds far and wide.

Evidence for the human use of chillies leads us first to southern Mexico where archaeologists working in the Tehuacán Valley have found indications that chillies were harvested from wild plants (and may even have been cultivated) as early as 7000BC. Archaeologist Richard Stockton MacNeish and his team worked from 1960 to 1970 on what became known as the Tehuacán project, during which time they discovered some of the first known evidence of domesticated chillies, maize, squash, tomatoes and avocados.

In an independent study, a complete pod of the habanero type was found in the Guitarrero cave in Peru. It dates back to 6500BC and is the earliest known example of this species.

It is believed that Native Americans began to cultivate chilli plants between 5200–3400BC. In Mexico, the Aztecs used chillies to prepare a drink called *chicahuatl*, a thick mixture made of cocoa beans, chillies, corn and water, that was the ancestor of what we know today as chocolate.

The conquest of Europe

It was from the West Indies that chillies made the leap to Europe. In 1492 Christopher Columbus returned from his second trip to the New World during which he attempted to discover a westerly route to the East Indies. King Ferdinand and Queen Isabella of Spain had financed Columbus's expeditions in an attempt to break the Portuguese monopoly over the trade in black pepper, which at the time was worth more than its weight in gold.

Thinking he had reached India, he named the local inhabitants Indians and the chilli 'pepper', under the misguided assumption that it was related to 'black pepper'. Columbus, in fact, had discovered the Arawak who inhabited much of the Caribbean region at the time. They had cultivated the chilli, its local name being *ají*, a name still in use today for several varieties.

From Spain, the cultivation of chillies spread across Europe. Gonzálo Percaztegi is believed to have introduced the chilli pepper to the Nive Valley in the Basque region of southwestern France in 1523. When the Turks invaded Hungary in 1526 they took along chillies, thus firing the Hungarians' love of paprika. (The invaders themselves had probably been introduced to the chilli by Italian or Portuguese traders.) Within a century, the chilli had spread to India, Africa and the Far East along the trade routes frequented by Spanish and Portuguese merchants.

Right: Ristras of drying chillies decorate a doorway in New Mexico.

Stories from the New World

As Europeans travelled to Central and South America, they returned with accounts of how the Aztecs and Incas used and worshiped the chilli. In 1577 Father Bernardino de Sahagún completed the Florentine Codex, a handwritten encyclopaedia of Aztec culture in which he described how chillies were used at almost every meal. In 1609, Garcilaso de la Vega described how the Incas worshiped the chilli as Agar-Uchu (Brother Chilli Pepper), one of four mythical brothers who featured in the Incan creation story.

The Tabasco™ story

One of the first commercial chilli products, this thin, orange red, slightly sour sauce is still a market leader today. The story of Tabasco™ sauce began in 1865, when Edmund McIlhenny returned home to Avery Island, Louisiana, after the American Civil War. McIlhenny started experimenting with growing what was to become known as the Tabasco chilli. How it got this name is not known for certain – there are various scholarly suggestions, each as plausible as the other.

Avery Island was well-suited to growing chillies – in its hot, humid climate the crops succeeded. Meanwhile, Edmund developed the sauce we know today.

In 1868 he formed the McIlhenny Company, which by 1870 had received a patent for its tabasco-brand sauce. In 1872 an office was opened in England to handle growing demands from Europe. A number of other companies began using the name on their products and McIlhenny was forced to fight long legal battles, but in 1906 the McIlhenny company registered Tabasco™ as a trademark.

Today, Tabasco™ remains the most successful chilli sauce ever made. Although its simple recipe of chilli mash, salt and vinegar has not changed over the years, the bottles have evolved. The brand has been very successfully marketed – despite a number of variant sauces bearing the McIlhenny brand, the original still leads the way.

Collected and classified

In 1543, the German physician and botanist Leonhard Fuchs illustrated several varieties of chilli in *The New Herbal*. From the mid-1700s chillies entered the scientific mainstream. Swedish-born botanist Carl Linnaeus, one of the founders of the Royal Swedish Academy of Sciences, developed his method of classifying, ranking and naming living organisms that is still in use today. Linnaeus classified the chilli as the genus *Capsicum*. Thanks to him now distinguish *C. frutescens* (*Capsicum frutescens*), from *C. annuum*, *C. baccatum* and *C. chinense*.

Using the Linnean classification method, Philip Miller, botanist and chief gardener at the Chelsea Physic Garden at the time, identified *Capsicum angulofum* in his *The Gardener's and Botanist's Dictionary* in 1768. Unfortunately, the Dutch physician Nikolaus von Jacquin subsequently reclassified the species in 1776 as *Capsicum chinense*. It is not known why he decided on the misnomer *chinense* – he was nowhere near China at the time (collecting plants in the Caribbean for Emperor Francis I of Austria) – but the name has stuck.

In 1794, Spanish botanists Hipolito Ruiz and Joseph Pavon classified *Capsicum pubescens*, the hairy pepper, in their publication *Florae Peruvianae, et Chilensis Podromus*. The two were part of a botanical expedition, sponsored by King Charles III of Spain, that began in 1773 and ended with their return some 11 years later, after almost constant hardship. In his journals, Ruiz described over 2000 plants and some of their uses.

Carl Linnaeus

Pure capsaicin – the early science of the capsicum

By the 1800s, the art of extracting active ingredients from plants was being perfected. In the case of chillies it was the compounds that gave the pods their heat that were especially soughtafter. In 1816–17, noted scientists Henri Braconnot and P.A. Bucholz extracted what they called capsicin from a mash of chilli peppers and ether from which the liquid was then filtered and evaporated, leaving a thick reddish substence.

During the 1870s, the scientists Rudolf Buchheim and J.C. Thresh worked independently on the isolation of a pure extract of the pungent compound from the chilli pepper. In 1873 Buchheim named his extract capsicol, and just a few years later in 1876 Thresh isolated a crystalline substance he named capsaicin.

It was not until the 1960s, with the introduction of High Pressure Liquid Chromatography (HPLC) that science discovered that capsaicin was made up not from one, but from a number of discrete compounds; these compounds have been named capsaicinoids. For more information on what makes chillies hot and how the heat is measured, turn to Chapter 2.

Left: A chilli harvest in India.

Chilli commerce

Hungary is world famous for its chilli powders, which are known universally as paprika. There is an unusual museum dedicated to the history of paprika in the town of Szeged, which, with nearby Kalocsa, vies for the title of paprika capital of Hungary.

The paprika industry was transformed in 1859 when the Palfy brothers of Szeged developed a machine that could control the amount of capsaicin removed from dried chilli pods. The machine removed the seeds and veins and then ground the pods into powder, enabling the production of a consistently mild and sweet paprika.

In 1879 the French chef Auguste Escoffier used paprika from Szeged in the kitchens of the Grand Hotel in Monte Carlo. Escoffier's use of what became known as the Hungarian Spice made it indispensable in the foremost kitchens of Europe.

Nowadays, paprika comes in various types including mild, sweet, rose and hot, though often it is used simply to add colour to a dish. However, good-quality paprika has a subtle and mysteriously bittersweet flavour all its own.

Improving and protecting the stock

Fabian Garcia is a special name in the world of chillies. A professor at New Mexico State University, Garcia produced the first scientifically developed chilli in 1894. He aimed to produce a milder fruit that was more acceptable to the general public, with a predictable pungency, size and shape. The result was the New Mexico No.9, which, after its introduction in 1913, quickly became the most popular chilli among commercial growers in New Mexico, until it was superseded by the New Mexico No. 6 in the 1950s. The No.6 had the advantage of being only half as hot – at between 700 and 900 Scoville Heat Units (SHU, see page 28) – and producing a higher proportion of well-shaped pods without deep folds in the skin, thus making it easier to process. Before Fabian Garcia, chilli production in New Mexico had been a hit-and-miss affair – the quality and the heat of the fruits were very variable. His efforts to create a more consistent harvest turned chilli production into a major cash crop for this area.

Work at New Mexico University has continued, with Dr Roy Nakayama, and subsequently Dr Paul Bosland leading the development of commercial chilli varieties. With this support, the chilli business in New Mexico has grown in value significantly. Only in the last five to ten years has production started to decline as the cost of labour and other factors have favoured chillies harvested in elsewhere – China, Africa and India.

The development of chillies at New Mexico University has produced other notable achievements including the NuMex Big Jim, which is listed in the *Guinness Book of World Records* as the world's largest chilli, its pods growing to lengths of over 20cm (7.8in).

In 1999, *Institut National des Appellations d'Origine* (INAO), the body responsible for the licensing and granting of *Appellation d'Origine Controlée* (AOC) status, moved to protect the unique *Pimente d'Espelette* (Espelette Pepper) from imported competition. This protection, also often seen on wines, protects the uniqueness of a product and, at the same time, helps to maintain its quality. Each batch must be presented for approval before it is issued with a number. If specialist regional products are to survive, they will need this kind of protection and control.

The production of the official Espelette Pepper is now limited to just 10 communities in the Basque region of southwestern France, near the Spanish border. Since 1967, a chilli day has been held in Espelette – an annual celebration of a local harvest that has been grown here since Gonzalo Percaztegi introduced the chilli pepper in 1523.

The hottest chilli

Frank Garcia of GNS Spices in California, USA, developed the Red Savina habanero, which is listed in the *Guinness Book of World Records* as the world's hottest chilli pepper.

This chilli variety was discovered when pickers spotted a few red pods in a field of orange habaneros. The fruit was saved, and the plants grown from the original were rated at a blistering 577,000 Scoville Heat Units in 1994.

Into the future

We are currently in a second boom for chillies. The first was sparked by their discovery and introduction to the West, the second has been encouraged by cheaper travelling costs that enable chilli lovers to sample foreign delights and take them back home. We can witness this in supermarkets, which display an increased availability of exotic products due to the growing interest in regional cooking styles. A web search will produce any number of sites with information on how to grow chillies and has made chilli products, previously unheard of outside their native areas, available to a keen world market. Chilli festivals are becoming increasingly popular around the world, with annual showcases in the USA, Canada, UK, Australia, France and South Africa growing from strength to strength.

The chilli has changed from an exotic rarity to a common ingredient in many kitchens. More and more people are enjoying the many varieties that are available, each of which has its own distinctive characteristics.

Right: In the world's colder regions, greenhouse, or tunnel farming provides a stable environment for growing chillies.

The chilli effect

Capsaicin is an alkaloid that has neither flavour nor colour and is so robust that it can withstand prolonged periods of drying, freezing and heating without losing much of its original pungency. When pure capsaicin makes contact with the human skin it causes an excruciating burn, which is why laboratory personnel working with the crystalline alkaloid have to wear full body suits and face masks to prevent accidental contact or inhalation.

The capsaicin found in chillies irritates the pain receptors in the mouth and nose. As soon as the brain receives the pain message it causes the release of a chemical (substance P) to counteract the condition. Repeated stimulation of the pain receptors leads to a diminished sensitivity, which is why people who regularly eat chillies are far less subsceptible to chilli burns than those who don't.

It is a fallacy that men can tolerate hotter food than women. The ability to withstand a chilli burn has little to do with gender, but depends largely on the distribution of taste buds on the tongue.

Be warned: the consumption of exceptionally hot chillies can cause contact dermatitis. Luckily the damage is hardly permanent – our taste buds are rejuvenated regularly – but if you cannot stand the pain and your mouth is on fire, have a glass of cool milk.

Right: Thanks to Carl Linnaeus, a chilli such as C.annuum can be easily distinguished from other varieties.

Chilli anatomy

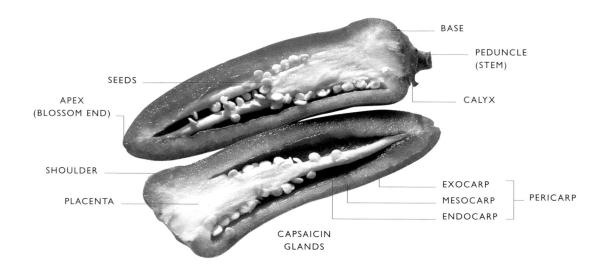

BASE

PEDUNCLE (STEM)

SEEDS

CALYX

APEX (BLOSSOM END)

SHOULDER

EXOCARP

MESOCARP

PERICARP

PLACENTA

ENDOCARP

CAPSAICIN GLANDS

Descriptions of chillies tend to use terms that are strange to us. To explain them, here is a picture of a chilli, cut and annotated so you can see what is what.

What makes chilli hot?

The heat in chillies is produced by chemical compounds called capsaicinoids. These are alkaloid compounds that are produced by glands in the placenta of the fruit. Capsaicinoids are only found only in the fruit and are not present in the stems or leaves of the plant. There are a number of different capsaicinoids, the best known of which is capsaicin, also the most pungent – in its pure form it is rated at 16,000,000 SHU.

Oleoresin Capsicum

If you look at the ingredient lists of some chilli sauces, you may come across oleoresin capsicum. This is not a type of plant, but a concentrated form of capsaicinoids extracted from the fruits. Mixing the chilli peppers with an organic solvent produces oleoresin capsicum. The resulting liquid is then heated so that the solvent evaporates, leaving behind an oily red mixture containing the capsaicinoids and colourants. Oleoresin (see page 9) can also be made from chillies that have little or no heat, simply to extract their colour for use as a food colouring. Manufacturers use oleoresin capsicum to colour and flavour products because it provides a controllable level of heat and colour to their product. It also has a long shelf life, unlike fresh chillies which must be processed fairly quickly before they begin to rot.

How hot is hot?

The heat of chilli peppers is rated in Scoville Heat Units (SHU), named after Wilbur Scoville, a chemist of the Parke-Davis pharmaceutical company. In 1912 Scoville developed a rather basic test designed to measure the relative heat of chilli pods. Scoville's rather simple method involved a panel of brave tasters and measured the point at which an extract of chilli could not be detected in water anymore. His method was unbelievably basic by today's standards: he blended pure ground chillies with sugar water, which was then tasted. The solution was increasingly diluted with sugar water until no heat could be detected. This amount of dilution became the now-famous rating: if the dilute consisted of one part extract to 600 parts water the chilli was rated at 600 SHU. As you can guess, the test was increasingly imprecise as the tasters gradually became accustomed to the heat.

Though SHU are still used today to indicate the heat of a chilli, the test has now changed to the more scientific and plausible-sounding High Pressure Liquid Chromatography (HPLC) developed in the 1970s for the separation of chemical compounds. Essentially, the technique provides us with a reading of the number – expressed as 'parts per million' (ppm) – of compounds present in a solution. As a rough guide to the number of Scoville Heat Units, we would multiply it by 15.

As with most things, the study of chillies is not an exact science – there are many factors that can affect their pungency. For example, hotter chillies tend to come from warmer climates. It has also been proposed that once the fruit is ripening, the heat can be increased by a reduction in watering. For these reasons, chillies are not given a single-value Scoville rating, but are normally sold with two values, showing the minimum and maximum values you can expect from the variety, as illustrated below (see *also* Chapter 3).

Right: A poblano ancho chilli.

How to cure a chilli burn

Capsaicin affects the pain receptors in the mouth, nerves that normally sense heat. Since capsaicinoids, the constituent components of capsaicin are not water-soluble, water will quench a chilli burn only temporarily. At worst it may increase it, because water simply serves to wash the capsaicinoids around the mouth. Various remedies have been suggested, but none can cure a chilli burn instantly because of the localized effect of capsaicin on the pain receptors in the mouth.

If you are really desperate have a glass of milk, or eat some yoghurt, or a slice of bread.

You could also consider downing a cool beer. Though it cannot really reduce the heat in your mouth, it does numb the rest of the body.

What is needed is yoghurt, milk, ice cream or – a favourite – fresh bread with a thick layer of butter. The fats and oils in these foods will quickly absorb the burn.

Chilli-based dishes are often served with rice or breads; while not as effective as oil at reducing the burn, they do help to soak up the capsaicinoids and clean the mouth. With continued exposure you will become more tolerant to capsaicinoids, and will be able to taste food again. Unfortunately, capsaicinoids are not broken down by the digestive system. Some experts recommend bananas to soothe any internal/external discomfort, but the best prevention lies in moderate consumption.

Right: Bell peppers have a zero SHU rating and are delicious in salads.

PEPPER/CHILLI	SCOVILLE UNITS (SHU)
bell pepper	0
poblano	1000 – 2000
jalapeño	2000 – 5000
serrano	8,000 – 20,000
de árbol	15,000 – 30,000
Tabasco	30,000 – 50,000
habanero	200,000 – 300,000
pure capsaicin	16,000,000

The medical uses of capsicum

Herbalist Dr John R. Christopher, an advocate of the medicinal properties of capsicum, used cayenne in many of his preparations and wrote several books about its use and benefits. Still available is the 600-page shopper called *The School of Natural Healing – The Reference Volume on Natural Herbs for the Teacher, Student or Herbal Practitioner*, which was his major work on the subject.

If Columbus and his crew had eaten some of the chillies they discovered on their journey, they would not have suffered from scurvy. This is because chillies are rich in Vitamin C. The US Department of Agriculture's National Nutrient Database lists red peppers as being endowed with 143.7mg of Vitamin C per 100g, while oranges contain only 45mg per 100g. Vitamin C is an anti-oxidant used by the body to soak up free radicals. Chillies also contain other anti-oxidants: lutein is found in red chillies, while alpha-carotene is found in yellow and orange chillies as well as peppers.

Over the years, a growing number of commercial products has included the ingredient capsaicin to relieve various aches and pains. Probably one of the very oldest is Sloan's Liniment Rub, originally developed for veterinary use, which was manufactured from 1903 by Dr Earl S. Sloan Inc.

The product contains oleoresin capsicum to produce a localized heat effect that causes increased blood flow and results in reddened skin. It was recommended for the relief of rheumatism and muscular soreness. Sloan's Liniment Rub is still available today, though these days Pfizer owns the brand. A German company produces a capsicum plaster that claims to be a 'remedy for lumbago', offering relief from pain, stiff muscles and cramps. Various other products use capsicum to similar effect, while others are designed to alleviate shingles, diabetic neuropathy and various other painful ailments.

Apart from claiming to be able to alleviate various physical conditions, chilli is also known to affect our mood. Capsicum causes the brain to release endorphins, natural painkillers that produce a feeling of wellbeing.

Right: Chillies are often dried spread out on the floor, as here in Stonetown, Zanzibar.

Pepper Sprays – non-lethal defence

Chillies have found a use in self-defence, and capsicum sprays are used around the world as a defence against animals. (The US Postal Service issues a spray to postal carriers to protect them from dog attacks, whose ingredients are modelled on the potent chemical make-up of chillies.) Originally developed in the 1960s by Professor James Jenkins and Dr Frank Hayes at Georgia State University, pepper spray was initially marketed as 'Halt Animal Repellent'.

Extra-high-potency versions have been developed to protect even against bear attacks, while milder versions were marketed as personal defence sprays. But these have now been declared illegal in many countries. Pepper spray causes swelling of the mucous membranes, an involuntary closing of the eyes and copious tearing, as well as coughing, and irritation and severe inflammation of the respiratory tract.

The spray is made from oleoresin capsicum which is mixed with alcohol or another organic solvent that acts as carrier. Pressurized gas is used as propellant. In 1989 the FBI published a report on the effects of pepper sprays: after three years of study and testing on over 800 willing subjects, the investigators reported no lasting medical effects, which led to the use of capsicum sprays by law enforcement agencies around the world.

The campaign against the use of such sprays has been vigorous and the debate continues: in 1997 Amnesty International condemned the US police in California for their use of pepper spray against peaceful protesters, calling it 'tantamount to torture'.

In the UK it is illegal to possess pepper sprays – even for self-defence, and there is currently a worldwide ban on bringing them on board aircraft.

Other uses

There are over 1200 patented products that include capsicum or chilli peppers. These include: insecticide, a spray to hinhibit web growth and discourage spiders, a boat anti-fouling coating, pain relivers and disinfectants.

Left: Chillies for sale in Port Louis, Mauritius.

Chilli identifier

Before we take a look at some chilli varieties let me explain a little about their family tree. Chillies belong to the *Solanaceae* family that has over 3000 members. Within this family, chillies come from the genus *Capsicum*, which includes five domesticated species and at least another 20 known wild ones. Each species is again subdivided into varieties. On the labels in garden centres and on seed packets you will see the varieties classified as follows: *C. chinense* red habanero. The *C.* is for the genus, *Capsicum*, while *chinense* denotes the species, and red habanero the variety.

There are thousands of varieties and more are developed all the time by universities and commercial companies around the world. Food companies are always looking for a more consistently shaped pod to make processing simpler, or a lower-heat jalapeño to make Tex-Mex dishes more palatable to a wider market. In some countries plant breeders can apply for PVR (Plant Variety Rights), which gives them some protection and allows them to control the commercialization of varieties they have developed.

Right: Chillies come in a multitude of shapes, sizes and colours – usually, the more attractive they are to look at, the hotter they are, so handle with care and experiment with caution.

The five domesticated species

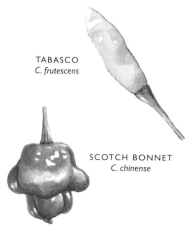

TABASCO
C. frutescens

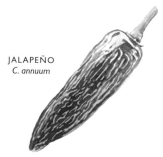

SCOTCH BONNET
C. chinense

JALAPEÑO
C. annuum

MANZANO
C. pubescens

C. frutescens
These have two or more purple or greenish white flowers at each node.
Examples: Tabasco chilli, bird pepper, japóne.

C. chinense
This species, which produces some of the very hottest varieties, was incorrectly named by the Dutch physician Nikolaus von Jacquin in 1776 who thought it came from China.
Examples: habanero, Scotch Bonnet.

C. annuum
This, the most commonly cultivated chilli, has hundreds – if not thousands – of varieties.
Examples: poblano, Anaheim, jalapeño, Peter Pepper, Cayenne, Thai, pasilla

C. pubescens
Named for the fine hairs that cover the underside of its leaves and the stems, its seeds are black and cannot be cross-pollinated with any of the other species. This limitation has probably kept the number of varieties of this species much lower than the rest. One of the most hardy species, the plants have been grown at higher altitudes and can withstand much lower temperatures, even light frost.
Examples: *rocoto, manzano*

CRIOLLA SELLA
C. baccatum

C. baccatum

The name *baccatum* refers to the small, berry-like fruit that is characteristic of wild chilli species. The varieties we are seeing today, however, are the result of centuries of careful cultivation and selective breeding. Examples: *ají amarillo*, *ají cereza*, brown *ají*.

Describing capsicum plants and fruits

The booklet published in 1995 by the International Plant Genetic Resources Institute (IPGRI) provides excellent descriptions of the growing conditions of capsicum plants, as well as the shape of their leaves, positions of flowers and the shapes and colours of fruit. This last point is especially interesting as it is what most of us are ever likely to see of the plant. If seed and plant merchants were to employ such a detailed method of description much confusion would be avoided and it would certainly help with identification.

Chilli identification guide

This guide presents the varieties you are most likely to come across, both fresh and dried. Familiarize yourself with their names – many chillies look so similar that trying to identify them by their fruit alone is a fool's mission. Scoville Heat Units are indicated where they are available and were correct at the time of going to print; the colour bar below each reading is an artistic representation of the pungency.

Aji Amarillo

Also variously known as yellow *ají*, *ají verde*, *ají fresco* and *ají escabeche*, these thin-fleshed Andean chillies ripen from yellow to orange. They grow to 10cm (3.9in) long and 3–4cm (1–1.5in) in diameter, tapering to a point and are often sold dried or as a powder. They are rarely found outside South America.

Species: *C. baccatum*
SHU: 40,000 – 50,000

| | | | | | | | | | |
|1|2|3|4|5|6|7|8|9|10|

Aji Cereza

The cereza, whose name means cherry in Spanish, grows wild in the Peruvian rainforests and attains a width of about 2–3 cm (0.7–1in).

Species: *C. annuum*
SHU: 70,000 – 80,000

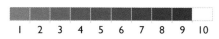

| | | | | | | | | | |
|1|2|3|4|5|6|7|8|9|10|

Aji Dulce

Dulce means sweet, and this is indeed a no-heat habanero. 'And what use is that?' I hear you cry. Wouldn't it be great to know what chillies really taste like before the heat kicks in? Well here's your chance – and if that doesn't appeal, why not impress your friends in the pub by eating this habanero whole in front of them without flinching? The fruits grow to 3–5cm (1–2in) long and 2.5–3.5cm (0.9–1.3in) in diameter, maturing from green, through orange to red when fully ripe. Be careful though: the seed can pick up the hot habit if it is crossbred with a more potent variety.

Species: *C. chinense*

Aji Limo

The fruit of this small Peruvian variety grows 4–5cm (1.5–2in) long and 2–3cm (0.7–1in) in diameter, starting at a very pale yellow and maturing through purple, yellow and orange to red.

Species: *C. chinense*
SHU: 50,000 – 60,000

Aji Limon

The fruits of this Peruvian chilli grow 4–7cm (1.5–2.7in) long and up to 2cm (0.7in) in diameter. They start as a greeny yellow and turn lemon yellow when fully ripe. Their thin flesh makes them ideal for drying and they add an interesting touch of colour when added to a string of chillies to form ristras (decorative garlands of dried chillies).

Species: *C. baccatum*

Aji Pinguita de Mono

Popular all over Peru but rarely available outside this country, these chillies are not grown commercially. The small fruits grow to between 1.5–2.5cm (0.6–0.9in) long and mature to a deep red.

Species: *C. annuum*
SHU: 70,000 – 80,000

Ammazzo

This is a very unusual looking Italian chilli whose fruits cluster together on the ends of branches in bunches of 8–15. The fruits grow to between 1–2cm (0.4–0.7in) in diameter, maturing from bottle green to red and very similar in appearance to the nosegay chilli, which also produces bunches of ripe red fruits.

Species: *C. annuum*

Anaheim

This mild green chilli is named after the Southern California city. The long fruits grow to between 15–20cm (5.8–7.8in) and are ideal for stuffing (*chiles rellenos*), grilling or pickling. They are mostly used when green, but become hotter when fully ripened to red. Anaheims have a tough outer skin, which can be removed by roasting and peeling (see Chapter 4). They are available both dried and fresh from specialist retailers or by mail order.

Species: *C. annuum*
SHU: 1,000 – 10,000

Ancho

The ancho is a dried poblano. It is normally smaller and lighter in colour than the mulato. Together with the pasilla and *mulato*, it forms part of the trinity of chillies used in the Mexican national dish *mole*. Anchos should be rehydrated in warm water for 15–20 minutes before use.

Species: *C. annuum*
SHU: 1,000 – 2,000

Antohi Romanian

This sweet pepper, originally from Romania, is now popular in the USA. The story goes that the seeds arrived with defecting acrobat Jan Antohi in 1991. The fruits grow to 10cm (3.9in) in length and up to 5cm (2in) in diameter. When ripe they are red, starting from yellow through orange.

Species: *C. annuum*

Apache F1

This dwarf hybrid chilli makes an ideal pot plant and can be displayed on the patio during the warm summer months in the northern hemisphere. It produces a good crop of fruits, 5–7cm (2–2.7in) long and 1.5–2.5cm (0.6–0.9in) in diameter at the shoulder, that turn red when ripe. Unlike some other highly developed varieties it keeps a good grip on its fruits, which can be left on the plant until needed.

Species: *C. annuum*

Bacio di Satana

The 'kiss of the devil' – a small, cherry-shaped chilli, 2–3cm (0.7–1in) in diameter – comes from Italy. The fruits ripen from green to red. Their thick walls make them ideal for stuffing and they are delicious stuffed with cheese and then baked or grilled in the oven.

Species: *C. annuum*

SHU: 40,000 – 50,000

Bangalore Torpedo

Growing to 60cm (23.5in) high, this Indian shrub produces long and twisted fruits that are 10–14cm (3.9–5.4in) long and 1–2cm (0.4–0.7in) in diameter at the shoulder. The fruits ripen from lime green to red, are good for pickling whole and are easy to dry.

Species: *C. frutescens*

NuMex Big Jim

The world's largest chilli pepper, growing up to 30cm (11.7in) long, was developed by Dr Nakayama at New Mexico State University in 1975. Big Jim produces long, thick, fleshy fruits. Developed for commercial production, it is also a popular chilli to grow at home as it yields an impressive crop.

Species: *C. annuum*

SHU: 500 – 1,000

Bird's-eye

This variety, whose diminutive size hides a searing heat, is also known as Thai, and tiny chilli. It can be found in most good Asian supermarkets, is simple to grow at home and it is not uncommon to get hundreds of fruits from a single plant.

Species: *C. annuum*

SHU: 100,000 – 175,000

Boldog

This genuine variety of Hungarian paprika produces smooth fruits that grow to between 10–15cm (3.9–5.8in) long and 2–4cm (0.7–1.5in) in diameter. They are the best choice for making your own paprika as the thin walls make them very easy to dry. For the best results, remove the seeds and placenta before drying.

Species: *C. annuum*

Brazilian Starfish

The unusual, flattened fruits that grow to only 2–3cm (0.7–1in) high but 3–4cm (1–1.5in) in diameter, with vertical ribs, look like short-tentacled starfish when viewed from above, hence the name. The fruits mature from green to bright red. This is a very interesting looking variety and makes an attractive ornamental plant.

Species: *C. baccatum*

Bulgarian Carrot

The stocky plants remain under 60cm (23.5in) in height and yield an impressive harvest that resembles small carrots, so it is not difficult to imagine how the variety got its name. A fast-ripening variety, they like full sun and the thin-skinned fruits, 7–10cm (2.7–3.9in) long, are good in salsas and chutneys.

Species: *C. annuum*

Capónes

Capónes are red jalapeños whose seeds were removed before smoking. The deseeding process is very laborious, which makes capónes quite expensive and means that they are not widely available.

Species: *C. annuum*

Casabella

This is a red or yellow thin-walled chilli that grows up to 4cm (1.5in) long. It has a low to medium heat and is good in stews and salsas.

Species: *C. annuum*

SHU: 1,500 – 4,000

Cascabel

The *bola* (Spanish for ball) chilli, which is known in its dried form as *cascabel* (Spanish for rattle), is a dark reddish brown fruit some 2–4cm (0.7–1.5in) in diameter and probably gets it name from the way the seeds rattle inside the dried fruit. It can be used in sauces, salsas, stews and soups.

Species: *C. annuum*
SHU: 1,000 – 2,500

Cayenne

There seem to be almost any number of cayenne varieties that range from miniatures to some that are almost 20cm (7.8in) long. The fruit is thin and tapers to a sharp point. Popular in Indian and Chinese dishes, cayenne pepper also been used in medical research: the fruits contain, among other things, anticoagulants that help to stop blood from clotting. It is also claimed that they increase the metabolic rate.

Species: *C. annuum*
SHU: 30,000 – 50,000

Charleston Hot

Related to the cayenne, but much hotter, the Charleston Hot yields thick-walled straight or slightly curved fruits up to 10cm (3.9in) in length and 2cm (0.7in) in diameter, ripening from green to yellow, then bright orange. Released in 1974 at Clemson University, South Carolina, this variety was developed to resist root knot nematodes. It is said that the peppers 'rival the heat of Charleston in August'. They are popular with gardeners but can be hard to germinate as they need temperatures around 26°C (78.8°F) for a few of weeks.

Species: *C. annuum*
SHU: 80,000 – 100,000

Cherry Bomb F1

The Cherry Bomb F1 is a good example of an early-yielding, small and compact chilli plant. The fruits grow up to 7cm (2.7in) in diameter and ripen from green to bright red.

Species: *C. annuum*
SHU: 2,500 – 5,000

Chi-Chen

The *chi-chen* produces bright red, thin-walled, very hot fruits, growing up to 7cm (2.7in) long and 1–1.5cm (0.4–0.6in) in diameter. Ideal in Chinese or Thai cuisine, they also make excellent ornamental plants. The fruits are easily dried, the thin skins become almost translucent and are very decorative.
Species: *C. annuum*

Chilhuacle Amarillo

Chilhuacle amarillo (yellow), also known as *chilaca* (the fresh form of the pasilla) hails from the Oaxaca and Chiapas regions of Mexico. The reddish yellow fruits, 6–8cm (2.3–3.1in) long and 3–5cm (1–2in) in diameter with broad shoulders, are used in *moles*, to which they impart a strong yellow colour. Available outside Mexico in dried form, generally only from specialist stores, they are worth hunting down for their excellent, slightly sweet-acidic flavour.
Species: *C. annuum*

Chilhuacle Negro

Chilhuacle negro (black) produces fruits that are heart shaped like bell peppers, 5–8cm (2–3.1in) long and the same across the shoulders, shiny and an attractive, dark mahogany colour. They have a wonderful, dark, liquorice flavour, and are used to make black *mole* – a speciality of in southwestern Mexico. Outside Mexico they can be found dried at specialist retailers.
Species: *C. annuum*

Chilhuacle Rojo

Chilhuacle rojo (red) also hails from southwestern Mexico. The fruits are dark red in colour and grow 6–8cm (2.3–3.1in) long and 2–4cm (0.7–1.5in) in diameter at the shoulders. This chilli is another staple of the Mexican national dish, *mole*. Outside Mexico, it can be found dried at specialist Mexican retailers.
Species: *C. annuum*

Chimayó

This fast-maturing variety is named after a town in New Mexico. The large, thick-fleshed chillies are similar to the Anaheim variety, but hotter, and grow to 20cm (7.8in) long. They mature to red, and can often be found dried and powdered in specialist stores. Like the Anaheim, the Chimayó is picked when it is green and used in stews, in salsas, or stuffed (*chiles rellenos*).
Species: *C. annuum*

Chipotle

The chipotle is not a variety at all, but is becoming the generic term for any smoked chilli. Ripe red jalapeños are most commonly preserved by smoking and drying. This is traditionally done in the field: chillies are placed on racks in a large pit, or smoke hut, and smoke from a nearby fire pit is channelled past the fruits. The fire, kept well-controlled and starved of oxygen, produces the smoke required to gradually dry the chillies. The versatile chipotle is used in many dishes as it imparts a wonderful smoky flavour with the characteristic mild heat of the jalapeño.
Species: *C. annuum*
SHU: 5,000 – 8,000

Choricero

This sweet, mild chilli from Spain, often found dried or as a paste, grows to 7–9cm (2.7–3.5in) long and 4–6cm (1.5–2.3in) in diameter, ripening from green to red. *Choriceros* are used to flavour the spicy *chorizo* sausage, as well as traditional rice dishes such as paella.
Species: *C. annuum*

Christmas Bell

This unusual Dutch chilli variety is uniquely shaped like a Christmas tree ornament. At between 5–7cm (2–2.7in) long and the same in diameter, the fruits are first green and then turn bright red when fully ripe. Use them in salsa and summer salads.
Species: *C. baccatum*

Costeño Amarillo

One of the few yellow chillies grown in Mexico comes from states of Oaxaca, Veracruz and Guerrero. They are often used in *mole amarillo* (yellow *mole*). The thin-fleshed fruits grow 6–7cm (2.3–2.7in) long and up to 2cm (0.7in) in diameter at the shoulders, tapering to a point.
Species: *C. annuum*

Criolla Sella

This Bolivian chilli produces cylindrical fruits 5–8cm (2–3.1in) long and 1–2cm (0.4–0.7in) in diameter, that ripen from green to orange when fully mature. The thin flesh makes them simple to dry, but the *criolla sella* is also good for adding to salsas or salads.
Species: *C. baccatum*

Cyklon

This variety of chilli is used to make dark-red paprika and comes from Poland. The fruits grow 9–11cm (3.5–4.2in) long and 2.5–3.5cm (0.9–1.3in) in diameter at the shoulder, tapering to a point. Mature fruits are thin-fleshed and hot and easy to dry. The best paprika is made after removing the seeds and placenta.
Species: *C. annuum*

Dagger Pod

With its long slender pod and gentle curve, it takes little imagination to see this chilli's resemblance to the sheath for a *kukri*, the short knife once used by Gurkha soldiers. The fruits grow to between 10–14cm (3.9–5.4in) long and 1–2cm (0.4–0.7in) in diameter, maturing from green, through orange to red when ripe. They are good in stews.
Species: *C. frutescens*

Datil

From St. Augustine in Florida comes the datil, a habanero-style chilli that is popular with the local Minorcan community, with whom it arrived in 1777 when they abandoned the slave-like conditions in the New Smyrna settlement. The datil is a prolific producer of dark yellow or orange fruits that grow to between 5–8cm (2–3.1in) long and up to 2cm (0.7in) in diameter. Like habaneros, they are very hot.

Species: *C. chinense*
SHU: 200,000 – 300,000

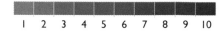

De Árbol

The de árbol is so-called because the bush resembles a small tree. It is related to the cayenne and is also known as bird's beak. The fruits are 5–10cm (2–3.9in) long, and deep red in colour. The thin flesh is easy to dry and often used to spice oils and vinegars.

Species: *C. annuum*
SHU: 15,000 – 30,000

Facing-Heaven

From the Sichuan province of China comes the Facing-Heaven chilli, also known as *Chi Ying Jiao*, so-called because its bright red conical fruits, which grow 8–10cm (3.1–3.9in) long, point to the sky. These chillies can be found in good Asian supermarkets.

Species: *C. chinense*

Fataali

The dangerous sounding *fataali* is a habanero relative from central Africa. The wrinkled fruits start green, maturing to bright yellow. They grow to between 6–9cm (2.3–3.5in) long and 3–4cm (1–1.5in) in diameter at the shoulder, tapering to a point. Like habaneros, these chillies are fiery hot and should be handled with care.

Species: *C. chinense*
SHU: 100,000 – 300,000

Filus Blue

A compact ornamental chilli with purple to almost blue leaves, the small egg-shaped fruits are first purple and eventually ripen to red. This variety is not noted for its flavour, but very good for adding heat.

Species: *C. annuum*

Ornamental Firecracker

Not to be confused with the Indian hybrid firecracker, the ornamental firecracker produces many small upright conical fruits, 1–3cm (0.4–1in) long, that ripen from purple to orange and red. Like other ornamental plants, this provides a most impressive display.

Species: *C. annuum*

Firecracker

This a compact plant produces a mass of cone-shaped fruits, 1–2cm (0.4–0.7in) long and around 1–1.5 cm (0.4–0.6in) in diameter, that ripen from white through purple to orange and finally red. This makes for a very showy display, but be careful: the fruit lives up to its name and is very hot.

Species: *C. annuum*

Fish

This chilli has variegated leaves and fruits that are green with yellow or white stripes and mature through orange to red. This variety is of African-American heritage, rare and unique. The chillies are popular in shellfish dishes.

Species: *C. annuum*

Fresno

Named after the town in California, the Fresno is easily confused with jalapeño or serrano chillies. The 5–8cm (2–3.1in) long, conical fruits are milder when green, ripening to red, and often used in salsa. A waxy skin and thick flesh makes them difficult to dry so they are best preserved by pickling or freezing.

Species: *C. annuum*

SHU: 3,000 – 8,000

1 2 3 4 5 6 7 8 9 10

Garden Salsa F1

Bred for flavour, not heat, this is a very versatile chilli, good in salsas and sauces. Its size, 18–22cm (7–8.6in) long and 3–5cm (1–2in) in diameter, makes the fruits good for stuffing, or for cutting into strips to be fried. The fruits ripen to red but are most often used when green, and are best roasted to remove the skin. To get a decent crop the plants need to be grown in a sunny position.

Species: *C. annuum*

SHU: 2,000 – 4,500

1	2	3	4	5	6	7	8	9	10

Georgia Flame

Deep red, thick-walled and crunchy, these fruits grow up to 15cm (5.9in) long and 5–6cm (2–2.3in) at the shoulder, and are good for producing hot salsa, for stuffing and baking. This variety comes from the Republic of Georgia.

Species: *C. annuum*

Goat's Horn

This versatile variety originated in Asia. It is a hot chilli that produces lots of twisted, glossy fruits – green maturing to red – up to 14cm (5.4in) long and 3cm (1in) in diameter.

Species: *C. annuum*

Guindilla

Outside Spain this popular chilli is most often found dried and strung up in ristras. The fruit is thin-fleshed, grows to between 7–12cm (2.7–4.6in) long and 1–2cm (0.4–0.7in) in diameter and is used for its excellent flavour. In Spain they are often used for tapas (light snacks or appetizers) when they are still green, the green pod not having acquired the pungency of the fully ripe version.

Species: *C. annuum*

Habanero

After the jalapeño, this chilli whose name means 'from Havana' is probably the best-known variety, its famed heat making it a favourite. They are grown extensively in the Yucatán Peninsula of Mexico and in Belize, where Marie Sharp's hot sauce is made. The fruits have a very attractive Chinese lantern-shape and can grow to 5–6cm (2–2.3in) long and 2–3cm (0.7–1in) in diameter. The most common varieties produce green fruits that ripen to orange. Habaneros need to be handled with some care. They are extremely hot and can easily cause blisters on the skin and tongue. Use them very sparingly and wear gloves when you are handling the fruits.

They are best grown in warm or tropical climates, take a long time to germinate and are considered the 'hothouse flower' of the chilli world. The plants require a lot of sunlight if the fruits are to ripen fully, and so they cannot be recommended for growers in the northern hemisphere. The variety is grown mainly as an annual as it does not winter well.

Common varieties include: red, brown, chocolate-brown and orange habaneros. See *also* Red Savina, datil, paper lantern habanero, Scotch bonnet, fataali and naga jolokia.

Species: *C. chinense*

SHU: 200,000 – 300,000

Habanero Red Savina

Red Savina is probably the ultimate in habanero-style chillies. In 1994 it recorded an amazing 577,000 SHU. None come hotter than this. The fruits grow up to 5cm (2in) long and 3–4cm (1–1.5in) in diameter. Developed after a lucky find by Frank Garcia of GNS Spices, it is much prized by sauce makers. The seeds are protected by Plant Variety Protection 9200255 and are only sold to home gardeners for their own use. Seeds from the crops must not be sold. The seeds can take a long time to germinate, so be patient. In cooking it must be treated with great care – just a few grams in a meal can be overpowering. You have been warned!

Species: *C. chinense*

SHU: 350,000 – 577,000

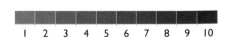

Hungarian Yellow Wax Hot

The fruits of this variety, which is also known as banana pepper, ripen to an orange-red, but are harvested yellow as this is when the flavour is best and the crisp flesh is ideal for use in salads and salsas. The fruits grow to 12–14cm (4.6–5.4in) long and up to 4cm (1.5in) in diameter.

Species: *C. annuum*
SHU: 2,000 – 4,000

Inferno F1

This Hungarian Wax hybrid produces masses of thick-walled, pendant fruits, 18–20cm (7–7.8in) long and 3–4cm (1–1.5in) in diameter. They start a greenish yellow and ripen to red, have an exceptional flavour and are good in many dishes.

Species: *C. annuum*
SHU: 2,500 – 4,000

Jalapeño

This is probably the best-known chilli in the world and has many different varieties – from the Tam Mild developed at Texas A&M University to the Gigantia, which can grow to longer than 12cm (4.6in). In America an industry has developed around this chilli, from growing and processing to selling, design and sales of equipment for the home gardener. The Campbell Soup Company even holds a US patent for a 'no-heat jalapeño'.

The jalapeño normally grows between 5–10cm (2–3.9in) long and 3–4cm (1–1.5in) in diameter with a very distinctive cylindrical shape. It is most often eaten green, but can also be used when a fully mature red. The fruit is often found with corky lines on the skin, but don't let this put you off – these are the best ones. The sweet heat from these fleshy chillies has made them popular around the world. Jalapeños are the staple of Tex-Mex cuisine, where they can be found on *nachos*, stuffed with cheese and coated in bread crumbs, or used in sauces and almost everything else that can be done with a chilli. Ripe red jalapeños that have been smoked are known as chipotles – this is a traditional Mexican method of preserving the crop.

Common varieties include: Gigantia (an extra large variety), Early (early fruiting variety), Tam Mild (smaller with less heat) and Sweet.

Species: *C. annuum*
SHU: 2,000 – 5,000

Jaloro

Developed and released in 1992 at Texas A&M University by plant virologist and breeder Ben Villalon, this is a uniquely yellow jalapeño. It was developed to be resistant to viruses, but still provides all the heat of its ancestor. It matures from yellow to red, but like the jalapeño is customarily used when it is still yellow and not fully ripe.

Species: *C. annuum*
SHU: 30,000 – 50,000

1 2 3 4 5 6 7 8 9 10

Jamaican Hot Chocolate

Another very hot relative of the habanero and Scotch bonnet, the Jamaican Hot Chocolate is believed to have originated from fruits discovered in the market in Port Antonio, Jamaica. When ripe these chillies are chocolate brown, about 4–6cm (1.5–2.3in) long and 3–4cm (1–1.5in) in diameter, with deep ribs and a wrinkled skin.

Species: *C. chinense*
SHU: 100,000 – 200,000

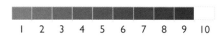

1 2 3 4 5 6 7 8 9 10

Japóne

Used in Chinese, Thai and Japanese dishes, japónes are red dried peppers, 3–9cm (1–3.5in) long and 1–2cm (0.4–0.7in) in diameter. They are similar to the de árbol and can be used in sauces and stir-fries.

Species: *C. frutescens*
SHU: 20,000 – 25,000

1 2 3 4 5 6 7 8 9 10

Joe's Long

This extremely long, red cayenne pepper grows to 20–30cm ((7.8–11.7in) but is only around 1.5cm (0.6in) in diameter. Thin-walled, it dries well but is ideally used fresh in Thai cooking, or for pickling whole in (long) jars.

Species: *C. annuum*

Jwala

From India comes the jwala, a prolific variety that produces many thin green pods, 10cm (3.9in) long and 1–2cm (0.4–0.7in) in diameter. They are often pickled green but mature to a deep red. Easy to grow, the plants are also quite attractive and can be likened to an umbrella because the fruits hang down below a canopy of leaves.
Species: *C. annuum*

Kashmiri Degi Mirch

From Kashmir, the northernmost state of India, comes the degi mirch. It is rare outside India as demand far outstrips supply; as a result other chillies are frequently passed off as the real thing.

About 5cm (2in) long and 2cm (0.7in) in diameter, the real degi mirch is a deep crimson, thin-walled fruit most often found dried or in powder form in Indian markets. Although not a very hot chilli, its sweet flavour makes it wonderful in milder dishes.
Species: *C. annuum*

Manzano

This chilli, also known as *manzana*, *rocoto*, *locoto*, *canario*, *caballo* and *perón*, is one of the few South American varieties not of the C. annuum species. The fruits have large, dark brown to black seeds and small hairs on their leaves and stems – all features unique to *C. pubescens*. Shaped like a small apple (*manzana*), each fruit is 2–3cm (0.7–1in) in diameter with thick flesh, initially green and ripening to yellow, orange and red, depending on the variety. The plants are resistant to lower temperatures than other species and are therefore ideal for cooler climates, but still require protection from frost.
Species: *C. pubescens*
SHU: 30,000 – 50,000

1 2 3 4 5 6 7 8 9 10

Mirasol (Miracielo)

This variety was named *mirasol* (looking at the sun), possibly because the pointed fruits grow erect. When dried the chilli is known as a *guajillo*, sometimes also called *travieso* (mischievous). The fruits ripen to dark red and reach about 12–16cm (4.6–6.2in) in length, 3–5cm (1–2in) in diameter. When dried they have an exceptionally tough skin and need long soaking before use. Less sweet, but a little hotter than the ancho, they are used in similar recipes – commonly in *chilaquile* (a casserole of tortillas, spicy tomatoes and cheese).

Species: *C. annuum*

Mulato

The mulato is a dried poblano, and generally larger and darker in colour than the ancho. Together with the pasilla and ancho, it makes up the trinity of chillies used in the Mexican national dish, *mole*. Rehydrate the dried fruits in warm water for 15–20 minutes before use.

Species: C. annuum

Naga Jolokia

In 2000, this variety was touted as the world's hottest chilli, rumoured to have beaten the previous record holder, the Red Savina, with a rating of 855,000 SHU (that's over 200,000 SHU higher). Many believe this 'record' was a hoax, and it has led to the seeds of other hot varieties being passed off as *naga jolokia*. Before, the Indian PC-1 was the hottest variety from the subcontinent, but – who knows – it may well turn out to be the *naga jolokia*?

Species: *C. frutescens*
SHU: 855,000

New Mexico No. 9

This, the first scientifically developed chilli, was created by Fabian Garcia of New Mexico State University and released in 1913. Its predictable pungency, as well as shape and size, soon made it the favourite with commercial growers in the area.

Species: *C. annuum*
SHU: 1,000 – 5,000

New Mexico Sandia

Another chilli produced by the prolific New Mexico University, this one developed by Dr Roy Harper and released in 1956, the Sandia is a cross between the original New Mexico No. 9 and an Anaheim-type chilli. It produces long, straight fruits 15–18cm (5.9–7in) long by 3–5cm (1–2in) in diameter at the shoulder, that ripen from dark green to bright red. They have less severe folds in the skin than Anaheims and have a flattened body.

Species: *C. annuum*
SHU: 1,000 – 2,500

NuMex Twilight

Developed by Paul Bosland and Jaime Iglesias in 1994 at the University of New Mexico, this ornamental plant produces purple fruits that develop through yellow to red when ripe. This is a compact variety commonly grown in pots that produces an impressive display of fruits.

Species: *C. annuum*

Orozco

The Orozco hails from Eastern Europe and produces large fruits up to 10cm (3.9in) long and 5cm (2in) in diameter, maturing from green to bright orange. Like some other Eastern European varieties, its fruits resemble carrots.

Species: *C. annuum*

Paper Lantern Habanero

Unusually shaped for a habanero, the pointed, elongated fruits of this variety ripen from lime green through orange to bright red. This plant is ideal for colder climates, where other habanero varieties can only produce a disappointing crop.

Species: *C. chinense*

Pasado

The Pueblo Indians of New Mexico traditionally roasted, peeled and dried the fruits of this chilli – both green and red – to preserve it for use in winter. This concentrated the flavours, making them sweeter and hotter with a lingering smokiness, excellent when used in soups and stews. *Chile pasado* means 'chilli from the past'.

Species: *C. annuum*

Pasilla

The pasilla (raisin) or *chile negro* (black chilli) is normally found dried or powdered. In its fresh form it is known as *chilaca*, but in California it is often confused with the ancho and may be sold as pasilla even in its fresh form. The fruits grow to 20cm (7.8in) long and 6cm (2.3in) in diameter with a very dark green skin that dries to brown, almost black. Their sweet, dark and smoky aroma lends a wonderfully rich flavour to sauces. Together with dried poblanos (ancho and *mulato*) it forms the trinity of chillies used in the Mexican national dish *mole*.

Species: *C. annuum*
SHU: 1,000 – 1,500

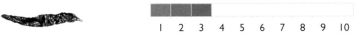

| 1 | 2 | 3 | 4 | 5 | 6 | 7 | 8 | 9 | 10 |

Peppadew

Johan Steenkamp discovered the Peppadew growing in the backyard of his holiday home in the Eastern Cape province of South Africa. The origins of this chilli are unknown, but growing and processing it has grown to a global business, with the pepper being exported around the world. The fruits are about the size of cherry tomatoes and have a sweet flavour with a mild to hot bite. The success of the Peppadew shows what can be done with a chilli that is well marketed. Seeds are not available commercially to the home grower, and no Scoville rating has yet been published.

Species: *C. annuum*

Pepperoncini

Originally from Italy, the *pepperoncini* produces contorted fruits some 7–10cm (2.7–3.9in) in length that are sweet and mild, ideal for salads and pickling. They mature through orange to red, but are mostly used when they are still green.

Species: *C. annuum*

SHU: 100 – 500

Peter Pepper

This pepper has a most distinctive shape – once seen, never forgotten. It is grown principally as an ornamental plant (that makes an interesting conversation piece), but its thin-walled fruit, 10–15cm (3.9–5.8in) long and 2–3cm (0.7–1in) in diameter, has a good flavour and is excellent in salsas and stir-fries. Though some companies have made commercial sauces from this pepper, they are not widely available.

Species: *C. annuum*

Pimiento

Not to be confused with the fruit commonly known as the 'red pepper, there are many varieties of pimiento including Perfection, Truhart Perfection and Super Red. The heart-shaped fruits grow 8–15cm (3.1–5.8in) long and 4–8cm (1.5–3.1in) in diameter. Commercially grown for canning or bottling, they are used for their colour and sweet flavour. Pimientos can be found bottled in supermarkets and are frequently sold as roasted peppers.

Species: *C. annuum*

Pimiento de Padron

A delicacy from Galicia in Spain, *pimientos de padron* are sweet peppers though about one in every eight can be hot. They are available from specialist shops and markets, but taste best fresh from the garden. To prepare them, heat up a skillet, add a good dash of olive oil, turn up the heat and add the fruit. Fry until they start to blister, then turn them into a bowl lined with a sheet of absorbent kitchen paper and add some coarsely ground sea salt. Eat them while they are hot, using the stem as a handle.

Species: C. annuum

Piquin

The piquin which grows wild in the highlands of Mexico produces hundreds of very tiny, very hot oval fruits – between 1–2cm (0.4–0.7in) long and a mere 5mm in diameter. Despite the minute size, piquins pack a real punch at up to 40,000 SHU. They are good in stews, but you may want to fish them out of your plate before you eat.

Species: *C. annuum*

SHU: 30,000 – 40,000

Piros F1

A reliable, easy-to-grow hybrid of the Anaheim-type, these plants grow to over 1m (3.28ft) in height and produce 18–20cm (7–7.8) long fruits that ripen from green to red.

Species: *C. annuum*

Poblano

The poblano has a large dark green, red or purple fruit up to 12cm (4.6in) long and 8cm (3.1in) in diameter. A dried poblano is known as ancho or *mulato*. Together with the pasilla this makes up the trinity of chillies used in the Mexican national dish *mole*. Due to their size, poblanos are also ideal for making *chile rellenos*.

Species: *C. annuum*

SHU: 1,000 – 2,000

Poinsettia

The fruits of this variety are arranged in a circle like flower petals and resemble a poinsettia bract once the green fruits have matured to deep red, hence the name. An ornamental plant, this variety produces thin upright fruits, 6–9cm (2.3–3.5in) long and 1–2cm (0.4–0.7in) in diameter that create an arresting contrast to the dark green foliage.

Species: *C. annuum*

SHU: 1,250 – 2,500

Prairie Fire

This tiny ornamental chilli plant grows to only 15cm (5.9in) high, but can spread to 30–38cm (11.7–14.8in). It produces hundreds of small, conical fruits – 1.5cm (0.6in) long and 5mm in diameter – that turn from yellow to orange and eventually a mature red. This is an excellent pot plant, ideal for a sunny location. Keep it in the kitchen for a ready supply – the hot fruit is great in stir-fries and in dishes that need a little boost.

Species: *C. annuum*

SHU: 1,000 – 1,500

Riot

This short compact plant produces a riot of 5–8cm (2–3.1in) long thin chillies that protrude upwards. The fruits turn from yellow to orange and bright red when ripe. Developed by Dr Jim Baggett of Oregon State University, this is generally an ornamental pepper, but the fruit is edible, so don't let it go to waste.

Species: *C. annuum*

Santa Fe Grande

The fruits of the Santa Fe Grande are most often sold and used in their unripe yellow form. If left to mature they will ripen to red. This is a large, waxy, thick-walled, conical chilli that grows 7–9cm (2.7–3.5in) long and 3–4cm (1–1.5in) in diameter, the fruits gently tapering to a point. The plants grow to 60cm (23.5in) in height. Commercially grown fruit are often canned or pickled, but they can also be eaten raw or cooked.

Species: *C. annuum*

SHU: 500 – 750

Scotch Bonnet

A relative of the habanero, the ferociously hot Scotch bonnet gets its innocent name from the shape of its fruit that resembles a tam-o'-shanter (a rimless woollen cap with a pompom that was worn in Scotland). Popular in the Caribbean, where they form the main ingredient in Jamaican barbecue seasoning and are also excellent in pickles and chutneys. The irregularly shaped fruit is somewhat smaller and squatter than the habanero, grows to between 2–4cm (0.7–1.5in) long and 1–3cm (0.4–1in) in diameter, and can be found in various colour combinations. Like the habanero, the Scotch bonnet can be hard to germinate and requires much sun if the fruit is to mature successfully. Common varieties include: Scotch bonnet red, Big Sun (larger than usual fruits, up to 6 cm (2.3in) long) and Burkina yellow.

Species: *C. chinense*

SHU: 100,000 – 300,000

Sebes

Originally from Czechoslovakia but also cultivated in parts of Hungary, sebes produces large, flattened, banana-style fruits 10–15cm (3.9–5.9in) long and 2–4cm (0.4–1.5in) in diameter that mature from green to bright orange and are ideal for stuffing or frying.

Species: *C. annuum*

Serrano

The serrano produces bullet-shaped fruits about 5–7cm (2–2.7in) long with a smooth skin. They are similar to the jalapeño in shape, but much smaller and more elongated. Due to their thin skin they can be used directly without any preparation, and are ideal for most dishes. Hotter than the jalapeño and with a sharper taste, the fruits ripen from yellow through green to red. There are a number of varieties, including the slightly larger purple serrano, which turns a deep purple instead of red.

Species: *C. annuum*

SHU: 8,000 – 20,000

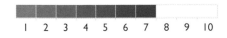

Shishito

The Japanese shishito is a small, wrinkled sweet pepper. It grows 8–10cm (3.1–3.9in) long and 2–3cm (0.7–1in) in diameter, and is used as a garnish for Japanese dishes. The peppers are picked when still green and will turn bright red when they are left to ripen.

Species: *C. annuum*

Super Chilli F1

This small, compact plant produces an abundance of very hot 5–7cm (2–2.7in) elongated fruits that ripen from green through orange to red. It was the All-American Selections winner in 1998, which is tantamount to winning a chilli Oscar for your variety.

Species: *C. annuum*

SHU: 20,000 – 40,000

Surinam Red

Both the red and yellow varieties probably originated in Surinam, South America, and both are extremely hot. In the Caribbean, the Surinam yellow is also known as the Madame Jeanette pepper. It produces the larger fruit and is closely related to the Scotch bonnet and habanero. Neither variety is recommended for growing in cool climates; they are hothouse plants outside the tropics.

Species: *C. chinense*

Szentesi Semi-Hot

The Szentesi semi-hot from Hungary produces fruits that are 10–15cm (3.9–5.8in) long and 3–6cm (1–2.3in) in diameter, maturing from yellow through orange to red. They are very good for stuffing and roasting, but are not easy to dry because of their thick flesh and firm skins.

Species: *C. annuum*
SHU: 1,250 – 2,500

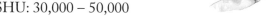

| 1 | 2 | 3 | 4 | 5 | 6 | 7 | 8 | 9 | 10 |

Tabasco

The Tabasco chilli is the key ingredient in Tabasco Sauce™. The plant, which grows to 1m (3.28ft) in height, is a prolific producer with up to 100 fruits that grow pointing upwards, which makes for an impressive sight. The fruits grow to between 3–4cm (1–1.5in) in length and about 1cm (0.4in) in diameter, starting a light yellow green and changing to red when ripe. Such is the global success of the hot sauce brand that the chillies used by the McIlhenny Company are grown, not only in Louisiana, but as far afield as Venezuela and Guatemala.

Species: *C. frutescens*
SHU: 30,000 – 50,000

Takanotsume

From Japan comes the takanotsume, a compact plant that grows upright and produces very hot clusters of fruits, 5–7cm (2–2.7in) long and 1–1.5cm (0.4–0.6in) in diameter, that are mostly found dried as flakes or powder.

Species: *C. annuum*

Tears of Fire

Expect a truly spectacular display from this prolific, ornamental conservatory plant. The fruit is initially green and then turns a rich brown before ripening to red. It can be cooked or used raw, but be careful: these chillies are hot.

Species: *C. annuum*

Tepin

The tepin, also known as the chiltepin, or bird pepper, grows wild in Mexico, the southwestern USA and some parts of Africa. The tiny fruit, just larger than a pea, is extremely hot. Germination is reported to take longer than that of domesticated chillies, but the plants will grow for many years if they are kept protected from frost.

Species: *C. annuum*
SHU: 40,000 – 50,000

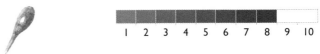

1 2 3 4 5 6 7 8 9 10

Thai Dragon F1

This variety looks very similar to the Super Chilli F1, except that the fruits grow pendant (hanging down). Thin-walled, they are 6–9cm (2.3–3.5in) long and 1–1.5cm (0.4–0.7in) in diameter, tapering to a point. The plant is easy to grow and produces hundreds of fruit that are easily dried for future use. Common in Thai cuisine, Thai dragons are good in stir-fries and can be added to the vinegar mixture when pickling onions to give them a little extra bite.

Species: *C. annuum*
SHU: 75,000 – 100,000

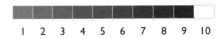

1 2 3 4 5 6 7 8 9 10

Tokyo Hot F1

A very prolific hybrid cayenne, the pencil-thin fruits ripen from dark green to red and grow up to 12cm (4.6in) long but are only 1–1.5cm (0.4–0.7in) in diameter.

Species: *C. annuum*

Chillies in the kitchen

For most people, 'chili' powder is their first experience with chillies in the kitchen. However, all is not what it seems. When buying commercial chilli powders it is best to check the list of ingredients and how the name of the product is spelled.

Commercial 'chili' powder (note spelling) does not normally contain just chillies but is an imaginative combination of spices that may include chilli, oregano, cumin, garlic and more.

'Chili powder' was developed in 1890 by William Gebhardt, a German immigrant living in New Braunfels, Texas, who created the spice mixture to make the preparation of the popular spicy meat dish known as *chili* (*chile*) *con carne* (chilli with meat) more convenient for the home cook.

Generic chilli powder can be made from a combination of different chillies, ground and mixed to provide a consistent level of heat. Generally, it is best to purchase a powder made from a variety you know. That way you can tell what to expect in the way of flavour and heat. You should be able to find cayenne pepper or jalapeño powder in most good supermarkets or grocery stores.

Right: Chillies can be added to almost any meal to spice up a bland dish or create an exciting taste sensation. Unless you are sure of the variety you are using, err on the side of caution and experiment carefully.

Storing fresh chillies

The best place for storing chillies is in the refrigerator (but not in a plastic bag, or they may rot), or in a cool dark cupboard. If you store them with fruit they will continue to ripen, and then rot.

Drying chillies

Dehydration is one of the simplest and oldest methods of preserving food items. The aim is to reduce the water content of the fruit and thus discourage the growth of bacteria and microbes. Chillies contain approximately 92 per cent of water, so dried ones will weigh a lot less than fresh ones do.

Dried chillies will keep for a year, after that they begin to lose their flavour. Keep the pods stored in an airtight container. I use Ziploc™ bags from which I remove as much air as possible. Good quality dried chillies should still be flexible, not brittle.

Air drying

Air drying is best done in a well-ventilated protected area (such as a screened verandah or an airing cupboard, for example), where the fruit is protected from pests. The process can take days or even weeks, depending on the conditions. Chillies have an elastic, watertight skin and will take a long time to dry whole. Use a skewer to make a few small holes in the skin to speed up the process.

Chillies are commonly dried after they have been strung together. If you choose to do it this way, be sure that the string pierces the stem of the chilli and not the flesh. Strings like these are called *ristra* in Spanish and are sometimes displayed in delicatessen shops.

Above Chillies can take some time to dry, depending on the weather conditions.

Sun drying

To sun dry your produce you need warm temperatures, low humidity and a constant breeze. After the drying is complete you will need to apply a method of decontamination to kill any insects and their eggs. Commonly, sun-dried products are frozen or baked to do this. Unless you have the correct conditions, this method is not recommended for the home.

Oven drying

To dry chillies in your oven, place them on a wire rack. Set your oven to its lowest setting (on some gas cookers just leaving the pilot light on will be enough). The temperature needs to be kept as low as possible, between 40–50°C (100–120°F), so you may need to keep the oven door ajar. The point is not to cook the chillies, as this will make them turn to mush when rehydrated. Fan ovens are excellent as they circulate the hot air, which speeds up the process. To make drying even quicker you can slice your chillies into rings and dry them on a baking tray lined with a piece of greaseproof paper.

Dehydrators

You can dry chillies at home without any specialist equipment; all you need is an oven. If you are planning to dry large quantities regularly, then consider investing in a domestic dehydrator.

~~~~~~

Rehydrating dried chillies

To rehydrate whole dried chillies, first clean off any dust with a tissue, or wash them gently in fresh water. Then place them in a small bowl and cover with warm water. How long they take to rehydrate will depend on the type of chilli you are using. Usually, the longer they are left to soak, the better. In most cases an hour is adequate. The water can be discarded.

Right: If you buy dried chillies like this, it is best to clean them before use.

Smoking chillies

Traditional Mexican smoked chillies (chipotles) are made from red jalapeños. Any chilli can be smoked, but the larger fleshy ones are best as they absorb more of the smoky flavour.

Smoking is an art form. A number of different smokers is available commercially; each works in a different way and requires more attention than you would expect. The simplest to operate is the Bradley Smoker which can be used for both hot and cold smoking and requires very little attention during the smoking process. Another type is the offset smoker that has a separate firebox. If you don't have a fancy smoker you can still smoke chillies in a kettle-style BBQ.

The aim is to dry and smoke the chillies over a long period of time. Remember that you do not wish to cook the flesh as it will turn into a pulp as soon as the chillies are rehydrated.

It is not advisable to use any of the variety of small stove-top smokers designed to hot-smoke meat and fish. These tend to get too hot and will cook the chillies before they are dried. However, they can still be used to smoke pre-dried chillies using the following quick cheat:

The cheat's guide to smoked chillies

1. The cheat's method is to buy already dried chillies (or dry your own) and then smoke them. They will not attain the same depth of flavour as the smoke will not have penetrated the flesh, but are an excellent substitute if you want to make your own chilli powder.
2. A second cheat, if you have a kettle-style BBQ, is to make a smoke pillow. Take hardwood chips (hickory, oak, or almost any fruit wood) and soak them in water for a few hours. Now take a piece of aluminium foil, approximately 600mm (24in) long and as wide, and fold it in half lengthways to make it double thick. Fold it

in half again lengthways and then fold over the short sides to make a little bag. Place the soaked wood chips in the bag and seal the long edge with a secure fold. Now use a skewer or small knife to make a number of small holes in one side of the pillow. Build a small fire on one side of your kettle BBQ and place the smoke pillow, holes facing up, against the coals. The pillow will generate smoke and protect the rest of the BBQ from the direct heat of the fire. If you make several smoke pillows you can replace them when they lose 'steam'. I find that smoking chillies for two or three hours imparts a very good flavour. Experiment, depending on how strong you want the flavour to be.

Cold smoking

To cold-smoke chillies for a full flavour requires time and patience. The fruit needs to be in the best possible condition – smoking is not what you do with leftover or damaged pods. A consistent source of warm smoke is required to dry and flavour the chillies. In a commercial smokehouse, the smoke generator is often separate from the smokehouse, a luxury we don't have for small-scale home smoking, so tend your smoker regularly to ensure that you do not cook your chillies.

With the exception of the Bradley smoker that can simply be switched on when it is needed, you need to prepare your smoker carefully and have extra fuel ready – this is going to be a long, slow process that can take up to two days. The final result should be pods that are hard, but still pliable, with a reddish brown colour.

You will need:
5–10kg (11–22lb) charcoal or coal briquettes
hardwood kindling
hardwood chips or powder (hickory is best, but oak
 or almost any fruit tree wood will do)
a kettle or offset BBQ
lots of fresh red chillies

Above: These chillies have been smoked to perfection using cherry wood.

DO NOT use softwoods or any wood that has been treated with varnish, polish, or preservatives. Similarly, do not use pine wood, and never opt for the wood of any poisonous plant, such as oleander. Charcoal or coal briquettes are the best heat source as they burn more consistently and controllably than wood. If you do wish to use wood, soak the wood chips or powder in water for a few hours before use; this is to ensure that they will smoke rather than burn.

In an offset smoker, build a small fire with charcoal or briquettes. If you are using a kettle-style BBQ, build a small fire on one side. then go and prepare the chillies.

1. Wash the pods to remove any unwanted pests and dirt.
2. Using a small skewer, pierce the chillies near the shoulder and again at the tip. This will speed up the drying process.
3. Place the chillies as far as possible from the source of the heat and close the lid of your BBQ.
4. Adjust the vents on your BBQ so that the fire continues to smoulder but does not go out (this is much harder than it sounds).
5. Check the BBQ every hour, and add more wood chips and charcoal as necessary.
6. Every few hours you will need to turn the chillies over and move them around on the grill.
7. Carefully inspect the chillies from time to time: you do NOT want to cook them.

Right: If you prefer, you can grind your chilli powder much finer than this.

Making chilli powder

Making chilli powder can be a dangerous sport if it is not done correctly, as I found out when I was developing our range of hot rubs and crisp flavours! Since then I have been seen wearing swimming goggles and an air filter – or what I call a painter's mask – when making up larger batches for sampling. It pays to remember that chilli powder can escape from almost any device you try to grind it in.

The best method is to use an ordinary blender (with a glass jug), with a sealing layer of cling-film wrap placed over the top before the lid is pushed on tightly. After grinding, remember that when you pour the powder into a storage jar, it will again become airborne, hence the need for goggles.

You can grind chillies as fine as you like. For very fine powders avoid grinding up the seeds as they make for a slight bitterness, but they are excellent in a coarsely ground mixture and make it look very attractive.

It is best to grind chillies that are very dry, otherwise they will clump. If you are unsure, place them in your oven/dehydrator until they are hard.

Pickling chillies

A traditional method of preserving food is pickling by using a pickling medium such as vinegar which contains a mild acid that prevents the growth of bacteria. Before pickling, chillies are often immersed in a brine (salt solution) to draw out some of the water that would otherwise dilute the vinegar and thus slow the pickling process. Adding salt to the pickling solution also helps to reduce the water content of the chillies.

Pickling solution

500ml (17½fl oz) water
500ml (17½fl oz) distilled vinegar
2 tsp non-iodized salt

Place the ingredients in a large pan and bring to the boil. Use a skewer to make a few holes at each end of the chillies if you intend pickling whole fruit, to allow the pickling solution to enter each chilli. Layer the chillies in a sealable jar and cover with the hot pickling solution, ensuring that they are completely covered.

The pickling process will take around two to three weeks. Pickled chillies should keep for at least a year if the jars are stored in a cool, dark place.

Please note that some recipes may require you to roast and skin the chillies before pickling them. This is because some varieties – such as the ancho, for example – have a tough outer skin that is best removed.

Above: Pickled chillies

Bottling chilli sauces

Making your own sauces and bottling them is easy. It is also a lot of fun to experiment with different ingredients. Store bottling jars in a clean, dry place until you are ready to use them. To ensure that your sauces keep, sterilize all jars or bottles each time before use by boiling them in hot water. Be sure to sterilize the caps as well and line each one with a seal (cut slightly larger than the lid) made of greaseproof paper.

Whatever the recipe you are preparing, all sauces should be cooked for a minimum of five minutes after reaching the boiling point to kill any bacteria before they have a chance to ruin your sauce.

1. While your sauce is bubbling away on the stove you must begin to sterilize the bottling jars you wish to use. Choose a pot that is deep enough to cover the selected sauce bottles with water completely.
2. Place a small wire rack in the bottom to keep the jars from resting directly on the base of the pot.
3. Stand the jars on the wire rack in the pot and fill with water, ensuring that the water fills all the bottles and covers them completely.
4. Turn up the heat and boil for at least 5 minutes.
5. Once the sauce is ready, remove one of the bottles from the water using tongs and fill it. Use a funnel to this so that you don't scald yourself, but remember that it, too, will have to have been sterilized in boiling water.

Ladle the sauce from the cooking pot while it is still boiling, directly into the funnel. It is advisable to use a clean towel to hold each bottle while filling it – again so that there is no chance that you might burn yourself.

When the bottle is filled screw on the lined cap and invert the bottle to seal it.

Most sauces made this way contain vinegar, lemon or lime juice as a base ingredient to raise the acidity level and prevent microbial growth. Bottled sauces should last up to nine months – the flavour will develop as they age.

Be suspicious when a bottle you have just opened makes a fizzing sound, bubbles or has an unpleasant smell. This is usually an indication that it was not sufficiently sterilized. In such cases it is best to discard the sauce immediately – do not even think of trying it.

Chillies in alcohol

For an unusual taste you could pickle chillies in alcohol. Preserving chillies in alcohol has two effects: it produces an interesting drink and also preserves the chillies for later use. I have a few bottles of chilli vodka that were sent to me from Canada. Each contains two 911 chillies. I kept them until the fruits started to turn a nice red colour; after three years I could wait no longer and tried it. WOW! I coughed and spluttered, and it was a few minutes before I was able to speak again. The concoction is far too strong to consume at room temperature, so now it lies in wait in the freezer until I find someone brave enough to try it!

I have also recently tried chilli sherry – and not for cooking, as I normally would – which makes a very pleasant drink. The secret, it seems, is to dilute the chilli sherry with six times its volume of normal sherry. The result is a fantastic, warming drink.

Freezing chillies

Frozen chillies do not reconstitute well when defrosted, because freezing ruptures the cells of the fruit and causes them to turn mushy. However, freezing is an excellent idea if you are going to cook with your chillies, for they lose none of their flavour or heat.

Blend excess chillies in a blender using a little water and pour the result into ice trays or even ice bags. When a little heat is needed just let one dissolve in the pan – as simple as frozen peas! Sauce and pickle manufacturers have freezers full of chillies in bags ready to be made into sauces and pickles, these are frozen on trays before bagging. In this way, the chillies are easier to separate when just a few are needed.

Previous page: Chutneys, jams and pickles – chillies are versatile.

The kitchen garden

Growing chillies is fairly simple and very rewarding: just a few plants can provide enough pods to keep most people going through the season. You can grow them in window boxes or in pots, have them standing in your kitchen or any other sunny spot. Although you can retain seeds from your plants, the ease with which chillies cross-pollinate means that you are unlikely to be growing what you expected. If you visit a seed producer you will see plants growing in their own tents in greenhouses. This is done as much to ensure that they produce pure single-variety seeds and cannot cross-pollinate with any neighbouring plants as it is to protect them from the elements.

If you are thinking of growing chillies from seed, I recommend that you get them from a reputable company that has some expertise in chillies. Seeds will keep for up to five years in a cool dry environment.

Growing from seed

If you have a garden with a sunny spot, get an early start and germinate your seeds as soon as possible. Spring is usually best, but enquire at your local nursery or garden centre if you are unsure of the best time to plant for your specific climate.

Chilli seeds require constant heat to germinate, so to ensure the best chances of germination they must be kept at between 25–30°C (77–86°F). Place the seeds in small pots or seedling trays, two to three seeds per pot, with a little good potting compost. Light is not important until the seedlings finally appear, but the soil must be kept moist, so don't put the trays in an airing cupboard and then forget about them.

1. Most seeds will germinate within 10 days, but be patient – some can take weeks. Pick out the strongest seedlings and place these in larger (8–10cm; 3–4in) pots. They will need to be kept in a warm light area: on a windowsill or in a warm conservatory is best.

2. Once the plants reach 10–15cm (4–6in) in height, you can repot them into larger containers.
3. Mix a little well-aged manure or compost into the soil to ensure that your chillies don't lack any essential nutrients. Alternatively, enquire at your local garden centre or nursery about a good plant food and use as recommended by the manufacturer.
4. If you live in an area that experiences mild winters then it is safe to leave your chilli plants outside – well-covered nonetheless. In cold areas move your chillies indoors and water sparingly but regularly. They may lose most of their leaves but should sprout again. Prune back old growth in spring and fertilize.

It is possible to grow chillies outdoors in the northern hemisphere, but remember that they need the same environment as tomatoes; a greenhouse or polytunnel will usually provide great results. In my conservatory I have a basic hydroponics system from Greenhouse Sensation (see page 122). The plants are placed into the system when they have grown to 10–15cm (4–6in) and the results have been excellent. The bottom line is: protection from the cold is essential.

Unless you just want fabulous and extravagant foliage, it is best to let the plants start fruiting before you provide them with a full dose of fertilizer. In the hydroponics system, plants enjoy a constant trickle of water and a proprietary nutrient mix. I initially start with a full dose, weaken it until the fruit is set and then return to a full-strength mixture.

For pot- or bag-grown chillies you can use feed that is recommended for tomatoes, watering each day and following the manufacturer's instructions (normally the plants need to be fed once a week).

Right: Polytunnel farming on a commercial scale.

Variety selection

Selecting which varieties to grow depends on where you live, what facilities you have available and, of course, your taste. Some plants can grow to a tremendous size and will require constant attention (as well as watering etc.). If you are looking for small compact varieties with a good crop of hot chillies, then Super Chilli F1 and Thai dragon are good starting points. Poblano and Anaheim chillies, on the other hand, will occupy more space and are not suitable for small home gardens.

Unless you live in a warm climate, habanero and the other super-hot varieties can be a bit disappointing. They can be hard to germinate and take a long time to fruit.

It may pay off to find a local expert who can give you advice about what varieties are best for the area in which you live. There are many chilli fans out there, and therefore many chilli-related websites that can provide seeds and give advice on growing them. Some of the best suggestions come from keen amateurs.

Left: Chillies make attractive container plants for the smaller garden and in the kitchen.

Cooking with chillies

In the course of my travels, my taste buds have been subjected to almost every culinary assault imaginable. Once, in Berkeley, California, I was invited to a Thai restaurant where each course was hotter than the one before. I survived, but only just, thanks to the valuable training received at my local Indian restaurant.

I was the target of countless ethnic dishes, and it seemed at times as though my hosts were vying with each to see who could do the most damage to my palate. Chilli peppers were the common denominator in all of the most memorable events.

At home I began to experiment with gusto. I once bought a tray of fresh chillies, washed them, cut them into rings and pickled them in vinegar – without protecting my hands. That night I could hardly move my fingers. Although I washed my hands again and again and lathered on copious amounts of cream, the discomfort lasted for nearly 12 hours. It was a lesson well learned.

Over the next 15 years or so I collected and tried many chilli recipes. I present you here with my favourite ones, together with some fine additions from fellow chilli fanatics Derryck Strachan, Chilli Pepper Pete and Andy Teo. In many cases no particular variety is specified, because I feel that that it is a matter of choice. If you like your food hot, then choose one of the more ferocious chillies, if you like it milder, then select a gentler burn.

Right: Chillies are an acquired taste, so unless you are used to them, or are feeling particularly brave, start with milder varieties and gradually work your way up to the seriously hot ones.

Spice mixes, sauces and salsas

Basic curry powder

I have eaten many curries and some have been really bad. The secret of a good curry is in the powder you use! Over the years I have tried most spice combinations and the recipe below is for a basic, but rich, curry powder. Feel free to adapt it, I have listed a number of options you may wish to add.

whole spices:
10 red dried chillies
10 tsp coriander seeds
6 tsp cumin seeds
3 tsp fenugreek seeds
2 tsp black mustard seeds
2 tsp black peppercorns
4 cardamom pods

ground spices:
1 tsp ground turmeric
1 tsp ground ginger

optional:
4–6 curry leaves
1–2 tsp white mustard seeds
1 tsp cinnamon
6–8 whole cloves
1–2 tsp caraway seeds
¼ tsp fennel seeds
½ tsp nutmeg
½ tsp horseradish powder

Remove stems and seeds from the chillies and then dry roast, together with all of the whole spices, in a thick-bottomed pan over medium heat. A high-sided pan is best as some of the spices will pop when they heat up. Dry roast for 5–10 minutes, keeping the spices moving so they don't burn. The aroma is great and the flavours will be much more intense.

Place the hot spices in a blender, or spice grinder and grind to a powder. You can also use a mortar and pestle. Now add the turmeric and ginger powder. Allow to cool before storing.

This mixture is best used within a few days, but can be stored in an airtight container in a cool dark place for several weeks.

Berberé

Berberé comes from Ethiopia. It is a dry spice mix and has become the basis for most Ethiopian cuisine. It is often made into a paste or sauce with the addition of oil, wine or water. *Berberé* makes a fantastic bread dip. It can also be used as a chicken marinade, either wet or dry, prior to roasting.

1 tsp allspice berries
3 tsp cardamom pods
16–20 cloves
4–5 tsp fenugreek seeds

2 tsp black pepper
1 tsp turmeric powder
4–5 tsp cayenne pepper powder
1 tsp salt

Dry fry all of the spices for a few minutes to bring out their special flavours, remembering to keep them moving all the time. Allow to cool and then grind with mortar and pestle, or in a blender, adding the salt, turmeric and cayenne a little at a time. This dry form of *Berberé* can be stored in the fridge in an airtight container until needed.

To make this into a paste add fresh ingredients such as finely chopped onions, ginger and oil, water or wine and blend to a fine paste. Store in an airtight container in the fridge, with a little oil poured over the top to keep air out and preserve it for longer.

Harissa

Harissa comes from North Africa and the Middle East. It is a smooth paste
made from dried chillies, garlic and olive oil, but can include other spices
such as caraway, cumin, coriander and salt. Available ready made in most good
delicatessen shops, it is very simple to make and adapt to your tastes.

2–3 large dried red chillies
2 garlic cloves
1 tsp caraway seeds
1 tsp cumin, ground

1 tsp coriander, ground
¼ tsp salt
olive oil

Soak the dried chillies in warm water for an hour or until reconstituted. Remove
excess water and dry with paper towel. Place in a blender with the garlic, caraway,
cumin, coriander seeds and a little salt and blend to a smooth paste. You can add a
little olive oil at this stage if required.

Place in a small jar and cover with a very thin layer of the olive oil. It will keep in
the fridge for a few weeks.

Chipotles in adobo

Chipotles are a staple in many Mexican dishes and every week I am asked to supply them. I have only ever seen them tinned so I am very pleased to have Derryck's recipe in my book.

6 chipotles
1 large onion, chopped
6 garlic cloves
6 tbsp cider vinegar
6 tbsp tomato ketchup
2 tbsp dark brown sugar

salt
450ml (¾ pint) water
1 tbsp vegetable oil
allspice, cinnamon, cumin (to taste)
3–4 tbsp lime juice

Place the chipotles in a pan with half the onion, 5 garlic cloves, cider vinegar, tomato ketchup, brown sugar, water, vegetable oil and the spices. Bring to the boil and then simmer over a low heat for about 20 minutes or until the chillies are soft and the mixture has begun to thicken.

Remove the chilli mixture from the heat and add the rest of the onion and garlic. Stir in the lime juice and season with spices and salt.

Keeps in the fridge for about a week.

Zhoug

This is a delicious Middle Eastern pesto, typical of Yemeni cuisine. Add it to soups, or use as salad dressings or condiment.

75g (3oz) parsley
50g (2oz) coriander, fresh
2 garlic cloves
1 tsp cumin, ground
1 tsp cayenne

1 tsp salt
1 tsp pepper
25g (1oz) fresh chillies (the hotter the better)

Put all the ingredients into a blender and mix well. Will keep for a week if stored in the fridge.

Mother's warm tomato chutney

This chutney recipe has been in my family for years, it is very simple to make and always turns out great.

2kg (4.4lb) tomatoes
4 medium size onions, finely chopped
500g (1lb) brown sugar
2 tbsp dry English mustard powder
1½ tbsp curry powder

1½ tbsp flour
1–2 tsp cayenne pepper
brown malt vinegar
salt as needed

Skin the tomatoes, cut into pieces the size of walnuts and sprinkle with salt (to draw out the excess liquid). Add the chopped onions and soak the mixture over night.

In the morning, pour off the liquid and discard, spoon the tomato and onion mixture into a pot and just cover with vinegar. Boil for 15 minutes.

Mix the dry ingredients (sugar, mustard powder, curry powder, flour, cayenne pepper) in cold vinegar to make a thick paste. Add to the tomato and onion mixture, stir well to mix and simmer over a low heat for about 45 minutes until thick, stirring occasionally.

Pour into sterilized jars and cover with lids while still hot. To allow the full flavours to develop, wait at least 2–3 months before you open a jar to enjoy your homemade chutney.

Lemon 'n lime fire chutney

This is a very sharp citrus-flavoured chutney, ideal on jacket potatoes or as a dip with curry. Instead of the limes and lemons you could use grapefruit and oranges.

6 limes
2 large lemons
500g (1lb) onions, finely chopped
50g (2oz) salt
500g (1lb) sugar
700ml (1½ pint) vinegar
2 tsp mustard seeds

2 tsp paprika
2 tsp ground cumin
1 tsp ground turmeric
20 hot Thai chillies, finely chopped in a
  blender or food processor
200g (16oz) raisins

Place the limes and lemons in a pan and cover with water. Bring to the boil and simmer for 2–3 minutes, then leave to stand until cool enough to handle. Cut the fruit into halves and squeeze the juice into a bowl, removing the seeds. Chop the remaining skin and pulp into small pieces with scissors or a sharp knife, mix in the onions and sprinkle with salt.

In a large pan bring the vinegar and sugar to the boil and simmer until all the sugar has dissolved. Add the chopped lime, lemon and onion mixture as well as all the dry spices, raisins and chillies, mix well and simmer for 2–3 hours stirring frequently until the mixture has reduced by about 50 per cent.

Pour into sterilized jars and seal while still hot. Your chutney will be ready to eat within 3–4 weeks.

The above recipe should make about 1.5l (3 pints) of chutney.

Jolly chilli pickle

These tasty pickles can be served with savouries as a snack and can also be served as a spicy side dish with any main meal.

1kg (2.2lb) large chillies
2 tbsp salt
1 tbsp turmeric, ground
2 tbsp black mustard seeds
125ml (½ cup) vinegar

2 tbsp garlic, chopped
500ml (1 pint) mustard oil
1 tsp fenugreek seeds
2 tsp nigella seeds
2 tsp asafoetida, crushed

Wash and dry the chillies. Remove the stems and cut up the chillies. Sprinkle with salt and turmeric, toss to mix evenly, cover and leave in the sun for two days. Soak mustard seeds in vinegar overnight, and grind in an electric blender with the garlic. Heat the oil and add the fenugreek and nigella seeds.

Stir and fry until fenugreek is golden brown. Add the asafoetida, stir, then add the blended mixture and the chillies together with the liquid that will have gathered. Simmer, stirring now and then until oil rises and chillies are cooked. Cool and pour into sterilized jars.

Burning hot mango pickle

This is oil pickle with mangoes is presented here the way they would make it in India. The mangoes are so unripe that the seeds are easy to cut through.

12 green mangoes
50 fresh green chillies
coarse salt
750ml (1½ pints) malt vinegar
2 tsp fenugreek seeds
25 garlic cloves, peeled
125g (4oz) fresh ginger root, sliced
60g (2oz) cumin, ground
60g (2oz) coriander, ground

1.25l (2 pints) mustard oil or vegetable oil
2 tbsp black mustard seeds
2 tbsp fresh curry leaves
2 tbsp fennel seeds
1 tbsp nigella seeds
1 tbsp turmeric, ground
1 tbsp chilli powder
salt

Wash and dry the mangoes and cut them into six or eight sections, through the seed. Cut the chillies in half. Sprinkle mangoes and chillies with salt; spread out on a large, flat basket and leave to dry in the sun for three days. Soak fenugreek seeds in some vinegar overnight, then combine with garlic, ginger, cumin and coriander in a blender. Blend to a smooth purée, adding just enough vinegar to facilitate blending. Heat the oil in a non-aluminium pan and add mustard seeds, curry leaves, fennel seeds and nigella seeds. When the mustard seeds stop popping stir in the turmeric, chilli powder and blended mixture. Fry, stirring constantly for a few minutes. Add the salted mangoes, chillies and remaining vinegar. Bring to the boil; reduce heat and simmer uncovered for about 30 minutes. Add salt to taste. Cool the mixture and bottle in sterile jars. There should be enough oil to cover the top of the pickle. Cover with non-metallic lids and always use a dry spoon when taking pickle from the jar.

Note: Use 500g (1lb) dried mango instead of the fresh mangoes in this recipe and bypass the salting and drying process.

Hot Juan's BBQ rub

The sauce will not burn in the intense heat of charcoal or gas grills and it's not only good for meat: it has been added to tomato soup, baked beans, steamed vegetables, garlic bread and homemade bread – all with excellent results.

1 tsp paprika (for colour not heat)
1 tsp garlic granules
1 tsp black pepper, finely ground
½ tsp dried basil

⅓ tsp cumin, ground
⅔ tsp chilli powder (it is best to select a single-chilli variety)
⅔ tsp salt

Place all the ingredients in a blender and blend to a fine powder. Lightly coat chicken, pork or fish and allow to marinate for an hour before use.

If you add two parts of sugar to one part of BBQ rub you can use the mixture to coat pork before roasting in the oven or in a BBQ using an indirect heat method. If you wish to use it on beef leave out the salt.

Cascabel and grapefruit sauce

This thin sauce makes a wonderful marinade for tuna or meat and will keep in the fridge for up to a month in a sealed container.

24 cascabel chillies
1l (1¾ pints) water
1l (1¾ pints) grapefruit juice
250ml (½ pint) orange juice

3 tsp allspice
1 tsp salt
3–4 cloves of garlic, finely chopped

Dry roast the chillies for 3–4 minutes, keeping them moving so that they do not burn. Add the chillies to the water and simmer for 20 minutes and then leave to cool.

Place water and chillies in a blender with half the grapefruit juice, as well as the garlic and allspice. Strain the mixture and then add the rest of the juices.

Quick enchilada sauce

This delicious enchilada sauce can be made ahead of time – it only takes about 15 minutes to prepare – and makes a tasty hot sauce for many meat recipes.

2 tbsp chilli powder
olive oil
1 large onion, very finely chopped
2 garlic cloves, crushed

3 tsp flour
250g (9oz) tomato passata (sieved tomatoes)
100ml (approximately ½ a cup) water

Lightly fry the onion and garlic in a little oil until translucent. Remove from the pan and set aside.

Reduce the heat to low. Add another 2–3 tablespoons of oil, then the flour, and mix well, using a whisk, until you have a fine paste that contains absolutely no lumps. Now add the chilli powder and tomato passata and whisk again.

Simmer for a few minutes to thicken, adding water if necessary. Return the onions and garlic to the sauce and simmer for another minute. The sauce can be used straight away or stored in the fridge for a few days.

Spoon over enchiladas, on pasta, or have it with bangers and mash – let your imagination lead you.

Fresh fruit salsa

It's a hot day – time to sit in the sun and enjoy a barbecue. But how about something a little different? This fruit salsa is great as a dip and can also be used on the BBQ. Spread some inside a whole fish before you grill it and enjoy a taste sensation!

1 large orange
1 large apple
1 kiwi fruit
1–2 onions, chopped
1–2 chillies, sliced and seeded

1 garlic clove, crushed
juice of one lime or lemon
a few mint leaves
salt and pepper

Peel and segment the orange, removing any unwanted seeds. Core and slice the apple. Peel and slice the kiwi fruit. Put all of the fruit into a blender together with the chopped onion, crushed garlic, chillies, lime juice and mint leaves.

Blend to a coarse but even consistency and then add salt and pepper to taste. Serve as a condiment for strong fish, or as a salsa for dipping.

Habanero hot sauce

This recipe is simple to make and the product can be bottled and stored.

12 habaneros
1 yellow pepper – roasted, skinned, seeded
  and chopped
1 onion, chopped
2–3 garlic cloves, chopped

125ml (½ cup) white wine or cider vinegar
6 tbsp lime juice
a little water

Sauté onions and garlic, add the yellow pepper and some water. Simmer on a low heat until the peppers have softened, then place in a blender with the habaneros and blend to a fine puree. Return to the pan, add the vinegar or wine, and lime juice, and simmer for a few minutes more. Store in clean, sterilized bottles in a dark, cool place.

Salsa cruda

This basic, uncooked salsa recipe makes a good base from which you can experiment with your own ingredients.

2–3 garlic cloves, chopped
1 small to medium onion, chopped
1–2 fresh jalapeños, chopped
5–8 tomatoes, cubed

3 tbsp fresh coriander, chopped
cumin, ground and roasted
lime juice to taste
salt and pepper

Place all the ingredients in a blender, holding back 2–3 tomatoes, and blend to a fine consistency. Place the mixture in a bowl, chop up the remaining tomatoes and add to the mix to give your salsa a more chunky texture.

Sambal oelek

From southeast Asia comes this sambal that can be used to add fire and flavour to all sorts of dishes, such as soups and stir-fries. I have seen variations with garlic, tamarind water and even lime juice – so be creative and experiment a little for a completely new taste.

10–15 cayenne or Thai chillies
dash of lemon juice
1–2 tsp salt

Using a mortar and pestle, pound the chillies to a fine paste, adding the salt a little at a time during the process. Add the lemon juice and mix. The paste will keep in the fridge for a few weeks, but can also be frozen for longer storage.

Teo chilli condiment

This is a simple but very tasty condiment my friend Andy Teo recommends. It can add that special 'something' to a meal of plain, steamed rice and chicken, or any other dish, for that matter.

2–3 Thai or cayenne chillies
a splash of sesame oil
white wine vinegar or lemon juice to taste
soy sauce to taste

Slice the chillies thinly, removing any loose seeds. Place in a small serving bowl and add the sesame oil, lemon juice or white wine vinegar, and some good-quality soy sauce until the mixture is to your liking.

Vizcaina

This traditional Basque chilli sauce is usually served with salted cod fish, but it
is also very good with chicken.

250g (½lb) onions
50g (2oz) choricero (or ancho) chilli, soaked
75g (3oz) parsley, chopped fine
3 garlic cloves

1 tsp Spanish paprika
250ml (½ pint) chicken stock
salt and pepper
olive oil

Sauté the onions in the olive oil until soft, then add the garlic, paprika and chilli
and simmer for a few minutes. Place in a blender with the stock and finely chopped
parsley and blend until smooth. Add salt and pepper to taste. Store in the fridge in a
sealed container.

Chilli Mustard

This semi-wholegrain mustard gets its heat from the chillies and mustard flour, and its sweetness from the rice wine vinegar. It is ideally served with cold meats and sausages.

50g (2oz) white mustard seeds
100ml (approximately ½ cup) rice wine
  vinegar

2 tbs olive oil
2 tsp mustard powder
2 tsp chilli powder

Soak the mustard seeds overnight in rice wine vinegar. Place this with all the other ingredients in a blender and blend until most of the seeds are broken.

Store in a small jar, best kept in the fridge.

Sambal Bajak

Sambals are cold savoury sauces, or dips, that are commonly served with Asian food. This particular one is a fried version that goes well with rice and can also be added to dishes that could use a little kick.

10 chillies
2 small onions, coarsely chopped
3 garlic cloves
12 macadamia nuts (or candle nuts)
1 tsp galangal powder
1 tsp shrimp paste

3 tsp sugar
125ml (½ cup) tamarind water
25g (1oz) coconut cream
2 tbs oil
salt to taste

Blend chillies, onion, garlic and nuts to a coarse paste. Add the galangal, shrimp paste and sugar and blend again. Heat the oil in a small frying pan and fry the mixture for a few minutes. Add the tamarind water, coconut cream and a little salt and simmer over low heat until the mixture starts to thicken. Place in a small jar and once cool store in the fridge.

Hot dishes

Chilli Pepper Pete's red bean soup

This delicious soup makes the perfect warmer on a cold day. Serve it on its own or with fresh bread and watch the winter blues disappear.

1 can red kidney beans, drained
1 large onion, finely chopped
2 tsp Mexican oregano
2 garlic cloves, crushed and chopped
500g (1lb) fresh tomatoes

2 soaked chipotles
2 soaked anchos
1 tbsp olive oil
salt and pepper
grated cheese for the topping

Roast the tomatoes at 180°C (356°F) for 45 minutes and sauté the onions in olive oil until soft. Add the garlic and simmer for a further few minutes. Place tomatoes, garlic, onions, beans, oregano and chipotles in a blender and mix until smooth. Pass through a sieve to remove any seeds and skin, place in a pan and cook over a gentle heat.

Fry the anchos in a little olive oil and cut in to strips. Add these to the soup and season with salt and pepper to taste. Spoon into bowls and top with a little grated cheese.

Watercress and poblano soup

The addition of a little roasted poblano gives this soup a subtle bite.

1 large bunch watercress, washed
4 potatoes, peeled and finely sliced
1 large onion, finely chopped
3–4 sticks of celery, finely chopped
2 carrots, finely chopped

1 poblano or ancho, roasted (see below)
olive oil to fry the onion
500ml (1 pint) chicken stock
sour cream (optional)

Saute the onion in a little olive oil in a large pan over low heat. When they turn translucent, add the potatoes, celery and carrots and fry for a few minutes before adding the chicken stock. Increase the heat to a simmer. Chop the roasted chilli and add. When the potatoes are done, add the watercress and simmer for a further 2–3 minutes. Remove from the heat and mix in a blender until the soup is smooth. Serve immediately with a dash of sour cream.

Chilaquile

This popular Mexican casserole provides a tasty way to use up old, stale corn tortillas by alternating layers of tortilla strips with layers of a rich spicy tomato sauce topped with cheese. The stack is baked in the oven and served with crème fraiche or soured cream.

6–8 corn tortillas
2 x 450g (1lb) cans of quality chopped
  tomatoes
1 medium onion chopped
100ml (approximately ½ cup) chicken stock

2–3 jalapeños or chipotles
200g (7oz) grated cheddar cheese or similar
oil for frying
crème fraiche or soured cream

First fry the tortillas in a little oil for about 10–15 seconds on each side to stop them from falling apart. The frying pan needs to be large enough to fit a whole flat tortilla. Set aside and drain on a paper towel. Fry the onion over a low heat until it becomes translucent.

Add chopped tomatoes, chillies and finally the chicken stock. Simmer for a further 5–6 minutes.

Tear the tortillas into strips and place a layer in a greased baking dish. Cover the tortillas with some tomato sauce and end with a layer of cheese. Continue in this way until you have used all the sauce and tortillas.

Place in a preheated oven at 180°C (356°F) for 15–20 minutes. When done, remove from the oven and serve immediately with a dollop of crème fraiche or soured cream.

If you like to experiment then vary this recipe by adding other ingredients such as beans, chicken or mince.

Doro wat

If you have made the *Berberé* (see page 92) then you'll want a traditional
Ethiopian dish to go with it. *Doro Wat* is a stew spiced with *Berberé* that
contains chicken and hard boiled eggs. There are many variations of this dish.
This is a particularly easy one.

400g (1lb) chicken breast, chopped into
small cubes
4 large onions, chopped
8 tsp Berberé, dry or wet
100ml (approximately ½ cup) oil or 150g
(5oz) butter
4 hard-boiled eggs
¼ tsp black pepper
¼ tsp garlic powder or fresh garlic

½ tsp ginger, fresh or ground
200ml (1 cup) red wine
500ml (2½ cups; 1 pint) water
salt
juice of one lime or lemon
variations:
2–3 tsp tomato puree
3–4 tsp peanut butter
chicken stock to replace the water

Place the chicken in a bowl and pour over the lime or lemon juice. Use a little of
the butter or oil in a large ovenproof pan to brown the onions. Add the rest of the
fat and all the spices. Simmer for a minute or two, stirring well. Add the wine and
150ml of the water, and boil for a few minutes, again stirring well.

Add the chicken, making sure it gets well coated, and gently cook for 30–40
minutes. Add more water if required, a little salt to taste and the boiled eggs. Stir
gently and return to the hob for a further 10 minutes at a low simmer or until the
chicken is done.

This dish is best served with flat bread. In Ethiopia, *injera* is eaten with it. If you
cannot find *injera*, then pita bread, tortillas or even a chunk of fresh crusty bread
makes a good alternative.

Creamy chicken curry

In this recipe I use coconut milk to give it a creamy texture, and red onions because they are milder in flavour (for the curry powder see page 90). This delicious curry is cooked slowly over a low heat – a large pan with a tight lid is best – and will take about 1–2 hours to prepare.

1–1.5kg (2.2–3lb) chicken pieces
  (drumsticks or thighs)
4 medium red onions, halved and thinly sliced
1 small cauliflower, cut into small florets
250g (9oz) mushrooms, cut into quarters
150ml (approximately ½ cup) coconut milk

4–5 celery sticks, chopped
4–5 tsp curry powder
50g (2oz) ground almonds
50g (2oz) raisins
4 cloves garlic, crushed
Olive oil for frying

Add a little oil to the pan and place over a low heat. When it is hot, add the onions, chicken and curry powder, turn up the heat and fry until the chicken has lightly browned.

Reduce the heat again to a low simmer and add all the other ingredients except the cauliflower. Simmer for about an hour and then add the cauliflower for the last 20 minutes.

Serve with rice or naan bread.

Mole poblano

This simple version of the popular and tasty Mexican dish does not call for any hard-to-find ingredients. You may also be able to buy ready-made *mole* sauce from a specialist retailer.

3 anchos

3 pasillas

3 mulatos

1 onion, finely chopped

3 garlic cloves, crushed

30g (1oz) almonds, toasted

30g (1oz) sesame seeds, toasted

1 tsp coriander, ground

5–6 tomatoes, peeled

60g (2oz) raisins

60g (2oz) dark chocolate

150ml (5fl oz) chicken stock

1 tsp cinnamon, ground

sunflower oil

1.5–2kg (3–4lb) chicken or turkey pieces

black pepper to taste

Remove the stems and seeds from the chillies before heating in a dry frying pan for a few of minutes. Keep them moving so that they don't burn, then rehydrate them in chicken stock for 10–15 minutes. Remove chillies from the stock, place in a blender with onion, garlic, sesame seeds, almonds, coriander, cloves, cinnamon and a little black pepper, and blend to a fine paste.

Slice peeled tomatoes in half, scoop out their seeds and chop fine. Melt the chocolate in a double boiler. Heat some of the sunflower oil in a heavy pan and fry the raisins until they puff up. Remove from the pan when they start to brown, add a little more oil if necessary and fry the paste you have made. Stir in the chicken stock you used to soak the chillies. Add the raisins and chopped tomatoes. Bring to the boil and gently simmer for 10–15 minutes. Add the melted chocolate and your sauce is ready to add to the chicken or turkey.

In a frying pan, seal the chicken or turkey in a little oil. Place in an ovenproof dish, cover with the sauce and bake at 180°C (356°F) for 30–40 minutes. Serve with plain boiled rice.

Tostadas

Most Mexican restaurants serve a version of *tostadas*, fried wheat tortillas with a layer of refried or kidney beans, chicken, lettuce, guacamole, soured cream and grated cheese topped with pickled jalapeños.

1 tortilla per person
1 can of refried or kidney beans, mashed
lettuce cut in to strips
1 chicken breast, cooked and flaked into
  pieces

guacamole
soured cream
cheddar cheese, grated
2 jalapeños (pickled or fresh), chopped
oil for frying

Fry the tortillas in hot oil, approximately 30–45 seconds per side. Flour tortillas will puff up when fried, but be careful not to let them brown or burn.

Place the fried tortilla on a plate and cover with a layer of beans (warmed if you like). Add the chicken, lettuce, good dollops of guacamole and soured cream, and top with the grated cheese and chopped chillies.

Hot Juan's fajitas

Fajitas were traditionally made from cheap cuts of beef, cut across the grain into thin strips and marinated to tenderize them. Nowadays almost any meat can be used. The fast cooking seals in the moisture and keeps the meat very tender.

2–3 chicken breasts, or 300g (¾lb) beef

3–4 tsp Hot Juan's Rub (see page 102)

1 red pepper, seeded and cut into strips

1 yellow pepper, seeded and cut into strips

1 large onion, finely sliced

oil

10–12 wheat tortillas

guacamole

soured cream

salsa

This recipe uses the dry spice marinade we created for barbecues. It is ideal for this type of fast high-heat cooking, but will not tenderize the meat. Cut the meat into strips, cutting across the grain of the meat. Place the meat in a bowl and sprinkle on some Hot Juan's, making sure you get an even coating.

Heat oil in a large frying pan and fry the meat over a high heat until it has browned. Set aside and fry the pepper and onion in the same pan. When they are almost done, return the meat to the pan and complete cooking. Doing this in two batches stops the pan from cooling down.

Spoon the meat in a warmed bowl and serve with warmed tortillas, guacamole, soured cream and salsa.

Hot coconut plantains

In culinary terms, 'plantain' refers to a green, unripe banana that is treated as and prepared like a vegetable. Sound strange? Try it, this recipe is superb.

2 green plantains
90g (3½oz) fresh coconut, grated
3 tbsp onions, finely sliced
1 or 2 green chillies, seeded and sliced

1 tbsp thick coconut cream
salt
dash of lime juice

Peel the plantains and boil them in lightly salted water until soft. Drain and mash, adding the coconut, onions, chillies and coconut cream. Add salt to taste and a dash of lime juice. Serve with rice.

Curried water spinach

Water spinach should be thoroughly washed as it grows in swampy areas. You can also try this recipe with ordinary spinach or cabbage.

500g (1lb) water spinach
2 tbsp oil
sprig of fresh curry leaves

1 medium onion, finely chopped
2 tsp dry chilli flakes
1 tsp salt

Wash water spinach, shake dry and break into bite-size pieces, using only the leaves and tender tips of stems. Heat oil and fry curry leaves and onions until onions are soft and brown. Add dried chilli, salt and the water spinach. Heat for five minutes. Serve with rice.

Cincinnati fiveway chilli

This is a real chilli spice fest, totally unlike the mince-and-chili-powder version familiar to many of us.

6–10 anchos
5–10 piquins
2 onions, finely chopped
5 garlic cloves
200g (7oz) braising steak, cubed
150g (5oz) black beans, soaked
1 small bunch coriander (root and stalks chopped and reserved; leaves finely chopped)
1 can tomatoes
2 tsp oregano
2 cinnamon sticks
2 or 3 bay leaves, fresh or dried

1tbs molasses
1tbs cider vinegar
500ml (1 pint) water

1 tsp each of the following:
paprika
cumin, ground
coriander, ground

½ teaspoon each of the following:
allspice
cayenne
cloves

Soak the black beans overnight. Drain, place in a pan of water and bring to the boil. Drain once again, cover with cold water and bring back to a boil. Reduce to a simmer and cook until tender – the timing could vary from one to two hours, check frequently.

While the beans simmer, remove the seeds from the anchos and soak them. Drain but reserve the liquid with its fine rich tobacco flavour. Pulp the chillies in a blender until smooth.

Slowly cook the onions until golden brown, but don't allow them to burn. Add the garlic until soft, then the chopped coriander root. Turn the heat to medium and add the meat. When the meat has browned, add the remaining spices and stir to coat the meat thoroughly. Sauté gently for a few minutes, but keep stirring all the while to stop the spices from sticking and burning.

Add the chilli puree and their soaking liquid, as well as the tomatoes. Drain the beans, rinse and add, along with the water.

Place in an oven dish and bake in a medium-hot oven about 2–3 hours. Check occasionally and add more water to prevent your dish from burning – it may develop quite a crust if you like it like that. The meat should be tender, almost dissolving and the beans soft and velvety.

Add molasses or honey if you like it with that bitter sweetness – I add some cider vinegar for a sour dash. If you want to add even more heat you can crumble the piquin chillies in at this stage, but beware! Serve with spaghetti, beans, chopped spring onions, or cheese and crackers.

Sichuan fiery beef

For an authentic taste try to find a good Chinese supermarket to supply some of the more unusual ingredients for this delicious recipe.

⅔ celery sticks or green beans
3 spring onions
500g (1lb) lean steak
1 tbsp Shaoxing wine (or sherry)
vegetable oil
1 tsp Sichuan pepper (there really is no substitute for this)

2 tbs chilli bean paste
500ml (1 pint) stock
2 tsp dark soy sauce
3 tbs flour mixed with 3 tbs water
a handful of dried chillies

Trim the fat off the beef and cut (against the grain) into thin strips. Marinate in the wine. Heat three tablespoons of oil in a wok until very hot.

Cut the chillies in half and fry in the wok along with the pepper. Sauté until fragrant and just beginning to brown (don't let them burn), then remove them but leave the oil in the wok. When the chillies are cool, chop very fine, almost to the consistency of paste, and keep for later. Reheat the oil.

Chop the celery, or green beans, as well as spring onions into pieces a few inches long and add to hot oil. As soon as they begin to colour, remove from the heat and reserve, keeping the cooking oil again.

Stir the flour mixture into the beef to make sure all the strips are well coated. Heat the wok once again, this time adding the chilli bean paste. Cook for a minute or so until the oil is red and fragrant.

Then add the stock and bring to the boil. When it boils vigorously, add the beef and bring back to the boil. Add the Shaoxing wine and soy sauce to taste. Leave for a few minutes, stirring occasionally. Then transfer to a serving dish and add the vegetables to the mixture.

When you are ready to serve, spread the chopped chillies on top of the beef mixture. Clean and dry the wok and heat up a tablespoon or so of oil until smoking hot. Pour this over the top of the dish, which will sizzle and spit dramatically. If you're quick you can bring it to the table while it is still sizzling.

Hot Juan's BBQ ribs

I have prepared racks of ribs more times than I care to remember. Each time I try something new and, so far, this is my best and simplest method.

Hot Juan's BBQ Rub (see page 102)
3–4 racks of pork ribs
1l (2 pints) apple juice or apple cider

5 tbsp cider vinegar
juice of one lemon
1 bottle BBQ sauce

Remove the inside membrane from the rack of ribs before you marinate it. With the tip of a knife locate the end of the membrane and lift a flap. Carefully gripping the flap with a dishcloth pull the membrane away from the ribs.

Now place the ribs in a large baking dish and pour over the cider vinegar, lemon juice and apple juice. Don't worry if it does not cover the ribs, we will be leaving them in the marinade for at least four hours in the fridge, and I recommend rotating them during this time.

After they have marinated drain the ribs (retain the marinade for future use) and coat evenly with Hot Juan's Rub. Massage in well.

Bake the ribs in a baking dish in an oven set to 120–150°C (249–300°F) for a few hours. Every so often you can spoon on a little of the reserved marinade.

When the ribs are ready it is time to cover them with the BBQ sauce and return them to the oven for 10 minutes or until they get sticky. Best served with French fries and coleslaw.

Chilli-brined pork chops

The aim of brining pork for six to 18 hours before cooking it is to make it much more succulent. With today's leaner pork cuts, we miss out on the fat basting the meat during cooking. Brining compensates for this loss in flavour.

240g (½lb) salt, or 60g (2oz) per litre
   (2 pints) of water
2l (3½ pints) water
2l (3½ pints) apple juice

dried chillies
6–10 peppercorns
2 garlic cloves

Pour the water and apple juice into a large pot. Add the salt, chillies, garlic and peppercorns. (Adding sugar or molasses to the brine mix will make it sweeter.) Bring to the boil and simmer for 10–15 minutes.

Cool, strain and then chill before using the brine to marinate your pork. You can brine almost any cut of pork, but the thicker cuts need to be left in the brine for longer.

To marinate the pork: place chops in a large plastic container, cover with the brine and place in the fridge for 4–6 hours. When you are ready to cook, rinse the meat in fresh water and discard the brine. Grill or BBQ as normal.

Hot Juan's patties

It may not be practical to make sausage at home, so prepare patties from this recipe instead, you could even shape the meat into a roll and coat with a little flour before cooking.

2–3kg lean pork
400–600g (14–20oz) pork fat (ask your
  butcher for this)

50g (2oz) Hot Juan's BBQ Rub (see
  page 102).

Mince the meat and fat, place in a bowl, sprinkle on Hot Juan's BBQ Rub to taste and use your hands to mix until all ingredients are evenly distributed. It may be wise to wear household gloves as the chillies could irritate your skin, especially if you have used a hot variety for your version of the Rub.

Other ingredients such as fresh or dried herbs can be added to your mixture to enhance the flavour. If you don't like it too meaty, you can add breadcrumbs or even boiled rice, but limit this to a maximum 5–10 per cent of the total weight of your meat mixture.

The flavour of the mixture will greatly improve if you are able to make it a few days before use, because the dry ingredients in the spice mix will have time to soak in.

Shape patties and roast on a barbecue over an open fire for the best results.

Chilli mackerel

This simple dish makes for a quick and easy single-pan meal. Serve it on a bed of rice or with fresh bread.

4 mackerel fillets

4 fresh red chillies, seeded and chopped

25g (1oz) blanched peanuts, unsalted

1 large red onion, chopped

2–3 garlic cloves, crushed

1.5cm (¾in) square of ginger, finely chopped

1 tsp turmeric

1 tsp lemon juice

50ml (4 tbsp) olive oil

75ml (6 tbsp) rice wine vinegar, dry sherry, or chilli sherry

175ml (¾ cup) water

Place all the ingredients – except the mackerel fillets and olive oil – in a food processor or blender and process until smooth. The mixture should not contain any large lumps, but must not resemble a paste.

Add oil to a flat-bottomed frying pan, pour in the mixture from blender and fry gently for a few minutes. Add the fish fillets and simmer on low heat for about six minutes, turning once.

Place fish onto plates and pour the sauce over it. You can serve this meal with French fries, rice, or fresh bread.

Spicy prawns (shrimp) with lime

Prawns (shrimp) are one of the most popular seafoods in the world. This recipe enhances their flavour and will delight your dinner guests.

30 raw prawns (shrimp)
2 tsp fresh ginger, finely chopped
1 tbsp fish sauce
2 tsp brown sugar
4 spring onions, sliced diagonally
4 red chillies, fresh
2 tsp galangal, finely chopped

1 tsp Thai pepper-coriander paste
2 tbsp peanut oil
3 tbsp coconut milk
1 tsp rice flour
salt
2 lime leaves or lime rind
red chillies, sliced for garnish

Shell the prawns, but leave the tail intact. De-vein and use a sharp knife to slit each prawn lengthways from the top. Place in a bowl and mix in ginger, fish sauce, sugar and spring onions. Marinate for 10 minutes.

Remove the seeds from the chillies. Purée in a blender with galangal, lemon grass, onion and Thai pepper-coriander paste.

Heat oil in a wok or frying pan. Add the paste mixture and stir-fry until fragrant. Add the prawns with marinade and simmer, turning constantly until they change colour. Remove the pan from the heat.

Mix coconut milk with rice flour and heat in a saucepan, stirring until it boils and thickens. Add salt to taste then pour into the centre of a serving plate or bowl. Place prawns on sauce and sprinkle with thread-fine strips of lime leaves or rind and fresh chilli.

Crab with chilli

This is an excellent seafood dish prepared in true, exotic Singapore-style to give your meal a very special touch.

2 raw crabs
125ml (½ cup) peanut oil
2 tsp fresh ginger, finely grated
1 tsp garlic, finely chopped
3 red chillies, seeded and chopped

3 tbsp tomato sauce
3 tbsp hot chilli sauce
1 tbsp sugar
1 tbsp light soy sauce
1 tsp salt

Clean the crabs. Remove hard top shell, stomach bag and fibrous tissue. Chop the flesh in 2–4 pieces, depending on size.

Heat a pan and add oil. When hot, fry the crab pieces until they turn orange or red, turning to cook on all sides. When done, remove, turn heat low and fry the ginger, garlic and chillies, stirring constantly, until soft and fragrant. Do not let them brown.

Add the tomato sauce, chilli sauce, sugar, soy sauce and salt. When the mixture boils, return crabs to the pan and simmer for three minutes. If sauce reduces too much, add a little water. Serve with rice.

Snacks and sweets

Chilli corn bread

This corn bread goes great with a barbecue and fresh salads. In winter it makes a perfect companion for rich tomato soup (any leftovers can be made into spicy *croûtons*).

150g (5oz) finely ground polenta
150g (5oz) self-raising flour
4 tsp baking powder
¼ tsp salt
60g (2oz) caster sugar
1–2 tsp paprika
2 chillies, finely chopped
200ml (¾ cup) milk

300g (10oz) crème fraiche
2 medium eggs

optional extras:
100g (3½oz) strong cheddar cheese, grated
1 can sweet corn
mixed herbs

Lightly grease a medium-sized, round cake tin and preheat the oven to 200°C (400°F).

Mix all the dry ingredients in a mixing bowl and add the chopped chillies. In a separate bowl mix the milk, crème fraiche and eggs, then add to the dry ingredients and blend using a whisk or mixer.

Pour the mixture into the cake tin, place in the oven and bake for approximately 30–45 minutes. When it is ready the bread should be golden brown and firm to the touch.

For a different flavour, you can add either grated cheddar, sweet corn or a pinch of mixed herbs.

Coconut flat bread

This exotic flat bread is made with freshly grated coconut, though desiccated coconut moistened with a few tablespoons of cold water can also be used.

500g (1lb) fine rice flour
1 tsp baking powder
75g (3oz) coconut, freshly grated
2 tsp salt
2 tsp butter (use ghee if you can)

2 tbsp onions, very finely chopped
1 tbsp fresh chilli, finely chopped
1 egg, beaten
500ml (1 pint) water
ghee or oil for cooking

Mix the flour, baking powder, coconut and salt in a bowl. Rub in the butter, stir the onions and chilli through, and then add egg and water to make a dough. Leave to rest for half an hour.

Take egg-sized pieces of dough and pat between floured hands or roll lightly on a floured board to the size of a saucer. Cook on a hot stove in a preheated heavy frying pan lightly coated with oil.

Serve with curries or sambals.

Devilled omelette

If you are tired of the old mushroom-and-cheese, cheese-and-ham, ham-cheese-and-tomato variations, then try this spicy breakfast surprise.

4 eggs
1 tbsp cold water
salt and black pepper
1 tbsp butter or oil

3 tbsp chillies, sliced
3 tbsp onions, sliced
1 tsp dill, chopped

Beat the eggs and add cold water, salt and pepper. Heat half the butter in a pan and fry the chillies and onions until soft. Cool the mixture, then stir it into the eggs together with the dill.

Reheat the pan, adding the remaining butter, and pour in the eggs. As the eggs set around the edge of the pan, draw the mixture to the centre, tilting the pan so the raw egg runs to the edges. Fold and serve.

Empanadas

These small pastry turnovers can have a sweet or savoury filling. We are going to cheat and use prepared shortcrust pastry, but if you wish to make your own pastry then use chicken stock instead of water to mix your dough. You'll get a more authentic flavour that way.

150g (5oz) beef mince
150g (5oz) turkey or chicken mince
1 large onion, chopped
1 red pepper, skinned, seeded and chopped
1 garlic clove, pureed
2 chillies (fresh or rehydrated), finely chopped or pureed

pinch of cloves, ground
pinch of cumin, ground
1 tbsp tomato puree
salt and pepper
1kg (2lb) shortcrust pastry
oil

Fry the onion and meat in a pan. Add the chillies and spices and fry for about five minutes. While the meat is simmering, roast the red pepper, remove its skin and seeds and chop into small pieces. Add to the pan, together with the tomato puree. Simmer until enough liquid has evaporated so that the mixture will not run when put into the pastry parcels.

Roll out the pastry on a floured surface until it is an even thinness of about 3mm (1/8in). Cut out as many 9–11cm (3.5–4.2in) circles as you can (normally 15–20). Place enough of the filling on the circles so that you can still close the pastry by folding it in half. Dampen the edges of the pastry before sealing and pinch the edges together using your fingers, a fork or a special gadget.

In a deep fat fryer, large pan or wok heat 3–4cm (1.5in) of oil to 180°C (356°F). Remove finished pastries from the oil once they are golden brown, and drain on a paper towel. Serve with salsa or hot chilli sauce.

Gyoza dumplings

Provide chilli sauce, soy sauce and wasabi as dips.

250g (1/2lb) white fish, skinned and filleted
juice of four limes
2 tbs of rice wine vinegar
a handful of chopped coriander
1 chilli, chopped

1/4 white cabbage, chopped
1 small leek, chopped
flour
dumpling skins (Gyoza skins)

Place the fish, lime juice, rice wine vinegar, coriander and chopped chilli in a bowl and marinate for 2 hours in the fridge.

Place the fish and marinade in a blender. Chop roughly and add the white cabbage and the leek. Blend to a chunky paste.

Flour a work surface or chopping board, place the Gyoza skins on the surface and put a teaspoon of the mixture in the middle.

Wet the edge of one half of the circle with your fingertips and then fold the dry side onto the wet side and squeeze the edges of the dumpling together. Pinch four points into the edge of the pastry and then, on the underside of each point, wet one half of the point only. Press the two sides together and you have a crease.

Drop the dumplings in boiling water in small batches. When they rise to the surface, fish them out with a slotted spoon and drain on a paper towel. Then heat some oil in a frying pan and fry them on one side until golden brown.

Serve with chilli dipping sauce.

Flaming eggs in soy

This is one of the many varied ways of preparing eggs in Asia. Indulge yourself with this spicy meal that will make your mouth (and eyes) water.

6 eggs
3 tbsp oil
1 medium onion, sliced thinly
2 chillies, sliced
2 tbsp brown sugar

3 tbsp water
2 tsp instant tamarind pulp
1 tbsp fish sauce
coriander leaves

Boil the eggs until hard. Then remove from the heat, and cool them by running cold water into the pot. When cooled, remove the shells and dry them. Pierce each one with a toothpick and fry until golden and crisp. Drain on paper towels.

Pour off all but a tablespoon of the oil. Heat the pan again and stir-fry the onion and chillies until the onion is golden and slightly crisp. Then drain.

Mix the brown sugar, water, tamarind and fish sauce. Stir the mixture over low heat until slightly thick. Pour the sauce over the eggs and sprinkle with the fried onion and chillies.

Garnish with coriander leaves and a chilli flower. Serve with rice.

Hot Juan's potatoes

These make a great change from normal roast potatoes, and if you cut them
into thin slices instead of wedges they are great with dips.

3 tsp Hot Juan's BBQ Rub (see page 102)
150ml (¾ cup) olive oil
3–6 potatoes (medium size)

Mix the olive oil with Hot Juan's BBQ Rub. Peel and slice the potatoes. Parboil and
drain, then place in a mixing bowl and pour the oil mixture over, mixing until the
potatoes are coated. Leave to marinate.

Pour a little olive oil in a roasting pan and preheat in oven set to 200–220°C
(390–430°F). When hot enough, remove the pan from the oven, add the marinated
potatoes and return to the oven. Roast until golden and crispy, turning once or twice
if you wish.

Pakora

This tasty, traditional Indian snack is probably the most commonly eaten treat, sold by street vendors and enjoyed all over India.

250g (½lb) chickpea flour
125g (5oz) onions, chopped
250ml (1 cup) milk
125ml (½ cup) water
½ tsp sugar
½ tsp salt

2 chillies, finely chopped
2 tsp coriander, ground
1 tsp cumin, ground
1 tsp turmeric, ground
500ml (1 pint) sunflower oil

Place all the ingredients – except the oil – into a bowl and mix well. Heat the oil and place teaspoon-sized balls of batter into the hot oil. Fry until browned and repeat until the batter is used up. Serve with curry and rice.

Stuffed anchos

This is another classic contribution from Derryck at the Ashburton Cookery School.

4–6 anchos
3 or 4 tomatillos, chopped
one small onion, chopped
2 tomatoes, chopped
125ml (½ cup) crème fraiche

a handful of grated cheese (such as cheddar)
flour, plain
2 eggs, separated
oil for frying

Slit the anchos and remove the seeds, then toast them in a dry pan over medium heat for 30–90 seconds a side, before soaking in warm water for 10–15 minutes or until soft and pliable.

Meanwhile, heat some oil in a frying pan and fry the chopped tomatillos for around three minutes. Add the onion and cook for three minutes, then the tomatoes and cook for another three minutes. Stir in the crème fraiche and season. Cover and simmer until the mixture bubbles up, then remove from the heat. Beat the egg whites until they form stiff peaks, then stir the egg yolks in one at a time.

Heat enough oil in a frying pan to cover the chillies. Take the soaked chillies, carefully open the slit and stuff with cheese. Turn them in the flour and then dip in the egg mixture to coat. Drop them straight into the hot oil without splashing. Fry one or two at a time, browning on each side. Drain on a paper towel.

Lastly, reheat the sauce and pour it over the chillies.

Chilli chicken 'popcorn'

This is my homemade, improved version of a commercially produced product. It is very quick and simple to make. The batter needs to be kept cool; it is best used chilled from the fridge.

2–3 cooked chicken breasts
1 large egg
100ml (½ cup) water (cooled)
50ml (4 tbsp) white wine vinegar
80g (3oz) plain white flour

½ tsp mixed herbs
1 clove garlic, crushed
½ tsp chilli powder
¼ tsp black pepper, freshly ground
oil for frying

Whisk the egg, water and white wine vinegar together. Place flour, herbs, garlic, chilli powder and black pepper in a mixing bowl and gently stir with a whisk while adding the liquid. Mix well and store in the fridge ready for use.

Heat 3–4cm of oil to 180°C (356°F) in a deep fryer or large pan (wok). If you don't have a thermometer, the standard test is to drop a small cube of white bread into the oil and see how long it takes to brown (about 60 seconds is what we are looking for).

While the oil is heating, chop the chicken breasts into small cubes and mix them into the batter, making sure they are well covered. When the oil is hot, fry the chicken in small batches. Remove when golden brown, drain and cool on a paper towel.

The chicken 'popcorn' is great with dips.

Spicy cashews

These delicious nuts can be served as a savoury snack with drinks. They are very tasty and bound to keep you coming back for more!

500g (1lb) raw cashew nuts
oil for deep-frying
2 tsp chilli powder
2 tsp salt

Heat oil in a pan and fry the cashews. Stir constantly with a slotted metal spoon. When pale golden, remove and drain on paper towels (the nuts will continue to cook in their own heat even after they have been removed from the oil). When all the nuts have been fried and drained, sprinkle with a mix of chilli powder and salt. Toss well to distribute the flavours.

When cold, dust off excess salt and chilli powder (shaking nuts in a colander is a good way to get rid of excess chilli and salt) and serve. May be made a week or two before required and stored in an airtight container.

Hot cheese straws

Shop bought cheese straws are tasty but very expensive for such a simple product. Here is my version of this popular party food. The Cheese Straws are best when they are fresh, but then – don't worry, they won't have a chance to get very old.

250g (½lb) plain flour
¼–½ tsp English mustard powder
½–1 tsp chilli powder, finely ground (select your favourite variety)
150g (5oz) butter

150g (5oz) strong cheese, grated (cheddar is best)
water
salt and pepper

Preheat the oven to 200°C (400°F).

Sieve the flour, mustard and chilli powder with a little salt and pepper. Rub in the butter until the mixture resembles breadcrumbs and then add most of the grated cheese. (Retain a little to sprinkle over the straws before baking.) Mix well, gradually adding enough water make a firm dough.

Roll out the dough 4–6mm (up to ¼in) thick on a floured surface. Sprinkle with the remaining cheese and cut into strips about 2cm (1in) wide. Place on baking parchment or a non-stick baking tray and bake for 10–15 minutes or until golden brown.

Cool on a wire rack and store in an air-tight container.

Chilli chocolate shots

From the beginning of history – well, at least since the Aztecs – chillies and chocolate have gone together. Today it would seem that sugar has replaced chillies, so how about a drink to revive the original pairing?

3–4 pieces of chocolate per serving (at least
  70 per cent cocoa content)
1 good pinch of chilli powder
100ml (½ cup) milk per serving

Melt the chocolate in a double boiler (3–4 pieces of per serving), or in a bowl that has been placed in a larger bowl of hot water. Add a good pinch of chilli powder and stir.

Warm the milk in a pan, add to the melted chocolate and stir well. (You may need to return this to the pan if not all the chocolate has melted.) Serve in espresso cups.

An alternative method is to use a microwave oven to heat the chocolate and then the milk before combining them. Stir well before a final heating in the microwave. For an interesting variation add a little espresso coffee to the mix, or even some brandy on a cold day.

Index

Picture credits

Published in 2012 by
New Holland Publishers Pty Ltd
London • Sydney • Cape Town • Auckland

First published by New Holland Publishers in 2006.
Paperback edition published in 2007. Reprinted in 2011.

Garfield House 86–88 Edgware Road London W2 2EA United Kingdom
1/66 Gibbes Street Chatswood NSW 2067 Australia
218 Lake Road Northcote Auckland New Zealand
Wembley Square First Floor Solan Road Gardens Cape Town 8001 South Africa

www.newhollandpublishers.com

ISBN 9781780093970

Publisher: Fiona Schultz, Publishing manager: Claudia dos Santos, Simon Pooley, Commissioning editor: Alfred LeMaitre, Copyeditor: Elizabeth Wilson, Designer: Stephanie Foti, Illustrations: Steven Felmore, Picture research: Karla Kik, Proofreader and indexer: Rod Baker, Design Concept: Stephanie Foti, Cover designer: Lorena Susak, Production Director: Olga Dementiev, Printer: Toppan Leefung Printing Ltd (China).

10 9 8 7 6 5 4 3 2

Keep up with New Holland Publishers on Facebook and Twitter http://www.facebook.com/NewHollandPublishers